Memoirs

The author.

Memoirs

Emmy Klieneberger-Nobel

ACADEMIC PRESS · 1980
A Subsidiary of Harcourt Brace Jovanovich, Publishers
London   New York   Toronto   Sydney   San Francisco

Academic Press Inc. (London) Ltd
24/28 Oval Road
London NW1

United States Edition Published by
Academic Press Inc.
111 Fifth Avenue
New York, New York 10003

Copyright © 1980 by
Academic Press Inc. (London) Ltd

All Rights Reserved
No part of this book may be reproduced in any form by photostat, microfilm,
or any other means, without written permission from the publishers

British Library Cataloguing in Publication Data
Klieneberger - Nobel, Emmy
　Memoirs.
　1. Klieneberger - Nobel, Emmy
　2. Microbiologists - Germany - Biography
　589.9'0092'4　　QR3.K54　　80-41231
　ISBN 0-12-414850-6

Set by DMB (Typesetting), Oxford.
Printed in Great Britain by
St Edmundsbury Press
Bury St Edmunds, Suffolk

Foreword

The fruits of intellectual effort, together with the striving itself, in cooperation with the creative activity of the artist, lend content and meaning to life.

Albert Einstein: *Out of My Later Years*,
Philosophical Library, 1950

FEW SCIENTISTS ARE PRIVILEGED to be on the starting line of a completely new field. It can be truly said that Dr Emmy Klieneberger-Nobel was a pioneer in mycoplasma research. While the initial discovery of this group of wall-free microbes occurred just before 1900, when French workers Nocard and Roux and their collaborators (Borrel, Salimbeni, and Dujardin-Beaumetz) described the micro-organisms causing bovine pleuropneumonia infection, progress in understanding the host distribution and pathogenicity of these organisms was exceedingly slow for the next forty years. A number of microbes with somewhat similar characteristics was isolated from animals and sewage between 1920 and 1940. However, research workers experienced considerable difficulties in working with these small, fastidious microbes and most experts were reluctant to connect the two groups: hence, the newly isolated organisms were referred to as pleuropneumonia-like organisms (or PPLOs). The real thrust in the field occurred in the late 1930s and 1940s when the research efforts of Dr Klieneberger-Nobel, and a few other pioneers (Derrick Edward at Wellcome Labs in England, John Nelson at Rockefeller Institute in New York, and Louis Dienes at

Memoirs

Harvard University) began to define the nature and distribution of these new organisms in a variety of hosts. Many of the rapid and fundamental developments that took place at this time, and the personalities involved, are described in this autobiography. Although the reader of *Memoirs* may gain some understanding of the circumstances that led to these developments, the author's modesty in delineating her major contributions requires that others emphasize her fundamental discoveries. Dr Klieneberger-Nobel provided the first conclusive evidence of an unusual stable bacterial variant while studying several mycoplasmas and bacteria from rats. She designated these variants as L-forms (L standing for Lister Institute) and outlined their similarity in cellular and colonial morphology, filtrability, and slow growth, to the mycoplasmas (or PPLO) then known. It remained for Dienes to show later that certain antibiotics, particularly penicillin, could induce the formation of these bacterial variants and that whereas the organisms were clearly derived from bacteria, they were distinct from the mycoplasmas. The sum total of these fundamental observations clarified the confusion among investigators as to what were mycoplasmas or L-forms and set the course for future research on mycoplasmas as a unique group of organisms distinct from other microbial forms. Dr Klieneberger-Nobel's active and creative research during this period also resulted in the isolation and characterization of three new mycoplasmas from rodents. She was the first to isolate *Mycoplasma pulmonis* strains from rats with bronchiectasis and to show that this organism was frequently associated with murine respiratory disease. Dr Klieneberger-Nobel was also the first to isolate *Mycoplasma neurolyticum* from mice and *Mycoplasma arthritidis* from rats with arthritis—events which contributed to the subsequent delineation of the role of these microbes and other mycoplasmas in acute infectious diseases. The amazing advances that occurred at this time received further stimulus in the early 1960s when researchers described the first mycoplasma to be identified as an agent in human respiratory disease (*Mycoplasma pneumoniae*), and again in the 1970s when mycoplasmas were discovered in plants and insects. Today, the rapidity of new observations on host distribution of mycoplasmas and their involvement in plant, insect, and animal diseases has completely out-distanced our wildest guesses of the future of mycoplasma research. One thing is clear: the fundamental scientific observations made by Dr Klieneberger-Nobel and other pioneers in the field have provided a solid and lasting foundation for advances not only in mycoplasma research, but in other endeavours in microbiology.

Foreword

Dr Klieneberger-Nobel has received many honours in her distinguished career. In 1967 she was elected an honorary member of the Robert Koch Institute. Recently, she was named as one of the first Honorary Members of the International Organization for Mycoplasmology, and that organization has established an award lectureship in her name to recognize other major and fundamental contributions to mycoplasmology. Dr Klieneberger-Nobel has also been a recent recipient of the Robert Koch Medal. This award of the German Robert Koch Stiftung is made to individuals for notable achievements in the field of microbiology.

A number of scientists and science writers has stressed the union of emotional involvement and intellectual discipline in shaping and forming the life of a scientist. When both of these components are present, the quality of that life and the research productivity or creativity that flows from these endeavours reaches unusual heights. The story Dr Klieneberger-Nobel tells in these pages emphasizes admirably the successful moulding of these attributes; while at the same time weaving a fascinating chronicle of her early life and scientific career. Her story has important lessons for today's young science students, particularly, in this time of emphasis on equal opportunity for women contemplating careers in science.

JOSEPH G. TULLY
National Institutes of Health (USA)

Contents

Foreword v

Acknowledgements xi

Introduction xiii

CHAPTER I
Forebears, Home and Youth 1

CHAPTER II
College Years in Göttingen and Frankfurt 26

CHAPTER III
Senior Teacher in Dresden 43

CHAPTER IV
Städtische Hygienische Universitäts Institut in Frankfurt 52

CHAPTER V
Germany during the Rise of the Nazis 70

CHAPTER VI
Life and Work in England 77

CHAPTER VII
My Last Working Period until My Retirement 108

Concluding Remarks 132

Publications 135

Acknowledgements

My sincere thanks are due to Professor Hans-Gerd Schiefer for procuring support for this publication from the German pharmaceutical firms Bayer AG, Leverkusen; Beecham-Wülfing, Neuss; Eli Lilly and Company, Bad Homburg; Pfizer, Karlsruhe. I should also like to thank Mr Francis A. Blake for his invaluable help with the translation of the German letters and the original German text.

To the memory of my mother, my brother Carl and my sister Anna

Introduction

Most people who were happy in their younger days and enjoyed their work as a hobby like to reminisce. It is interesting to consider that all races and all kinds of people have conceived ideas about an existence beyond their natural life on Earth. I am of the opinion that even for those who do not hold any beliefs in recognized orthodox religious dogmas it is difficult to comprehend the fact of death, the final end of existence—particularly the loss of a beloved person. We continue to dream of those who were once so dear to us as if they were still with us. When we are fully awake, but not occupied with work or leisure activities, we may daydream and then we talk in our minds with the beloved ones as if they were still in our presence. We know that nothing lasts forever, that everything is finite and that even the universe is in continuous transformation. The scholars tell us that our Earth did not always exist and that it will perhaps eventually unite again with the sun. How can we grasp that then even the music of Beethoven and the plays of Shakespeare will never be heard again? Because we cannot understand this finality we desire for ourselves our own little bit of immortality. We hope that something of us will be left when we have retired from the stage.

We look at our little trinkets, at our belongings and particularly at our books and decide to whom of our relations, our friends and colleagues, we are going to leave them so that they may remind them of us. We also think of the exciting events of our working days and our scientific discoveries (small though they may have been) and the sleepless nights they caused us.

I therefore intend to write about my past, and I shall include letters, some of them by prominent scientists whom I admired and who gave me their friendship. I address my writings to my family, my friends and colleagues, and to anyone who would like to read them.

CHAPTER

Forebears, Home and Youth

Wohl dem, der seiner Väter gern gedenkt,
Der froh von ihren Taten, ihrer Grösse
Den Hörer underhält, und still sich freuend
Ans Ende dieser schönen Reihe sich
Geschlossen sieht . . .

Goethe: *Iphigenie auf Tauris*

THE YOUNGER members of my family, I expect, will be interested to hear something about our common ancestors. I shall begin my story by relating what I know about them. My memories of our forebears do not go back very far. Of my grandparents on my father's side I only know that my grandfather, Joseph Klieneberger, was born in the year 1804 at Jungvorschütz and that he died in the year 1869 at Teplitz. He married Katharina Stransky, who was born in the year 1810 at Kwutusch and died in 1903 at Vienna. They lived in that part of Austria then called Bohemia. My grandfather was known to some people as a glove-maker and to others as a Rabbi and teacher. Probably he followed both callings. The Joseph Klienebergers had four children of whom my father, Abraham Klieneberger, born on 19th January 1833 in Raschowitz, was the oldest. He later changed his first name Abraham to Adolf, and was generally known as Adolf Klieneberger. His only brother was my Uncle Saemi (Samuel) and his two sisters were my aunts, Mrs Gellner and the unmarried Sophie Klieneberger. I remember that a telegram arrived one

1

night, greatly shocking my parents, informing them of the death of Uncle Saemi. My grandmother Klieneberger died at the good old age of 93 and, being myself then eleven years old, I can still remember when her death was announced to my parents. However, I did not know any of these relations personally.

My father visited his mother during her lifetime and his two sisters every year in Austria until he was eighty. I remember well when my father came to see my brother Otto and myself on his return journey from Vienna to Frankfurt at Göttingen in the year 1913. I was then a student and my brother registrar (Oberarzt) at the University Psychiatric Clinic. I was proud of my handsome 80-year old father. My Aunt Sophie sent me a golden chain-bracelet on my 18th birthday, which is still in our family. My grandparents on my mother's side both came from Hanau am Main. Grandfather Julius Hamburger was born on 6th March 1806 and died on 7th March 1884. He married Röschen Dilsheim, born on 10th March 1806, and who also died in the year 1884. My mother used to say: just like both my parents I am going to die at the age of 78. Yet when she had reached that age she never mentioned this again. She told me more than once that my grandparents Hamburger had been very nice and kind people and that grandfather was overjoyed when his grandson Otto (born 6th March 1879) had been given to him as a birthday present. I was always sorry that I (born 25th February 1892) had never known any of my grandparents in the flesh. However I knew quite well the brothers and one sister of my mother, namely my Uncles Heinrich and Louis and my Aunt Emma. Of my mother's cousins I knew particularly well Uncle Heinrich and his sister Aunt Emma Dilsheim, and also Adolph and Jenny Hamburger, the parents of my intimate friend and schoolmate Liesel Hamburger. All these relations lived in our neighbourhood at Frankfurt. Uncle Heinrich Dilsheim visited us every Sunday afternoon after the death of Aunt Emma, with whom he had shared a flat. He was a good man and I was rather fond of him.

My father would have liked to have had a higher education; but money was lacking. When he was eighteen he had to join the Austrian Army as he could not afford a substitute, as was then customary in well-to-do families. He was a well-built young man and no doubt the sporting outdoor life in the cavalry, in which he served, agreed with him. He became a sergeant. When he left the forces at the age of thirty-eight, with twenty years service, he was offered a clerical post, but an office job did not appeal to him and instead he became a travelling wine merchant. He attained the age of ninety and always kept his fine military bearing.

Forebears, Home and Youth

After some years with a wholesale wine merchant he acquired his own business with a cellar in the Stiftstrasse in Frankfurt and employed a cooper, Herr Jung, often mentioned by my parents. Frequently I went with my mother to this roomy cellar, which one entered from the street through a trapdoor. There I saw the numerous vats of wine and smelled that odour characteristic of all wine cellars. Several times a year my father travelled through Germany visiting his customers, and I expect he obtained good orders. From my parents' conversation I gathered that he was a particularly welcome guest in some of the big estates in North and East Germany. On his returns he often brought back special purchases such as the fine Meissen dinner and coffee service (for 18 people) which graced our dinner table on all festive occasions. In winter he wore a fine brown cloth coat for travelling, lined throughout with beaver and trimmed with a beaver collar; he also wore a matching round beaver cap. All this must have been very serviceable on those East Prussian estates in winter. My father was a most conscientious business man whose books—later with my mother's help—were kept faultlessly to the smallest detail. I am sure Justizrat Julius Hamburger, my mother's father, could have had no objection when the handsome 41-year-old business man asked for the hand of his 26-year-old daughter Sophie in marriage, in May 1874 at Hanau.

My father gradually saved a modest sum of money—modest according to the standards of the time—however sufficient to buy the roomy and well-situated corner house at 51 Reuterweg in Frankfurt in the year 1895. It was surrounded on three sides by a garden. I can well remember that my mother went with me and our maid from the Böhmerstrasse, where I had been born, to the house in the Reuterweg to take the measurements of the rooms. There were four storeys in the new house and we moved to the one on the first floor. We had in the front three well-appointed rooms with parquet floors covered with carpets from Smyrna in various colours and patterns. The first of these rooms on the left of the hall was a roomy sitting-room which made a warm impression with its dark-green wallpaper, its large bookcases, a sofa and an elegant lady's desk which I was permitted to use when a student. It was also the room in which the large Christmas tree was erected with its many candles, its glass baubles and tinsel. Tables with a display of presents, as well as the tree, remained there during the week between Christmas and the New Year. A double door led from the right side of this room to the 'salon', which contained small upholstered easy chairs and a settee, all covered in brown velvet. Our guests were received in this room. Another double door on its right led into the large dining-room in the middle of which was an extension table that could easily seat twelve people, a number frequently entertained by my mother at festive afternoon or evening social gatherings. From my twelfth year onwards I was allowed at these parties and I greatly enjoyed slices of the goose liver and particularly the dessert, a 'Charlotte Russe' which was always served on these occasions.

The dining room had a French window on the front side which opened up onto a small balcony. There, together with our dear Paula, the faithful maid of twenty years, I stood on New Year's eve punctually at 12 p.m.; all church bells were ringing and we shouted a loud "Prosit Neujahr" down to our neighbours, who had all come out of their houses and were standing in the street.

The three rooms mentioned, all situated at the front of the house, were joined at the right side by a room called 'das kleine Zimmer' (the little room). There we had our meals on ordinary days, and there also I did my homework under the watchful eyes of my dear Mama, and played there afterwards. As a child I was allowed into the 'good rooms' only when we had visitors. At the corner of the house, towards the back was the roomy bedroom of my parents, adjoined by the so-called bathroom. This was a room of middle size in which I slept with my sister. A bath tub had been installed in it at the end opposite the iron stove. The beautiful back garden could be seen from its window and that of the kitchen situated to the right of it. A large part of the back garden was covered with lawn and a huge hydrangea bed. These hydrangeas were always in bloom in my memory. Tidy gravel paths surrounded the lawn and the flower bed. Jasmin and lilac bushes were growing on those sides of the garden adjoining neighbouring gardens. In the farthest corner of the garden loomed an enormous chestnut tree which was covered in white flowers every spring, and every evening in summer there cascaded down from its top the sweet song of a blackbird. In the neighbour's garden grew a big *Catalpa syringifolia* (a *Trompetenbaum*) with its trumpet-shaped flowers, and even as a child I knew that summer was nearing its end when the Catalpa was in bloom. The so-called 'Berg' (hill) was on the street side of the garden. It was surrounded by a brick wall towards the street and on the neighbour's side; several steps led up to it. A table and chairs had been placed on its top. It could be regarded as a nice secret place for an unobserved rest or a chat or for having tea or, more often on hot days, fruit juices brought down to us from the kitchen by dear Paula.

The part of the garden that led from the house in the front and on the

Forebears, Home and Youth

side had been made into a rose garden by my father, who loved plants and flowers; there were bush roses, standard roses and ramblers climbing up the garden fence. Father took great care of his roses; he gave a bunch of them sometimes to an honoured guest, but avoided with great caution cutting roses which still carried buds on their stems. All the gravel-covered garden paths were kept clean and tidy and the garden was regularly watered in summer. I had sometimes to perform this duty on hot summer evenings—the summers seemed to have been always hot in my youth. For a thorough watering a hose was fixed to a hydrant which supplied 'Main'-water, for it then was forbidden to use drinking water for the watering of gardens. After the wetness had thoroughly sunk in the garden breathed out a cooling humid atmosphere which gave relief to body and lungs and made one forget the hot and dusty air of the streets.

My father was very careful and exact in all his activities at business and at home. He wore exclusively mother's hand-knitted socks and only woollen 'Jäger' underwear. He also ate and drank in great moderation; for example he never touched any sausage because only dear God (*der liebe Gott*) knew what was inside, and he instructed my mother to buy only Prague ham because this was known to be the very best. Wine is hardly ever drunk in a wine merchant's because this abstinence preserves the fine discriminating taste of the wine merchant's tongue which plays so great a role in the testing of the new samples sent by the producers. Wine merchants came often to our home for testing sessions with my father. The samples were sent in small testing bottles. My father and his colleagues tested the samples by means of nose and tongue: the small amounts introduced into the mouth were spat out. Vats of the wines of those samples that had stood the test were then ordered from the producers. After these sessions a number of half-filled little bottles remained; they were passed on to my mother and on the following day we had for dinner a lovely sweet, called 'arme Ritter' with an excellent wine sauce. Only on the occasions when my father had invited a special guest for a meal did he go down into our cellar and come back with a dust-covered old bottle of a very special wine, the origin of which was related to the guest, and my father drank one glass of this delicious drink very slowly and with apparent delight. My father was of a cheerful disposition; a certain pleasure in living emanated from him. In spite of his wish to economize he did not wish my mother to be thrifty. He asked her more than once to buy herself a new hat and to have a new dress tailored at the dressmaker's; one did not buy off the hook in those days.

My father planned excursions from time to time or proposed a summer holiday in Switzerland. He sometimes came home from his club in a carriage and mother used teasingly to call him a spendthrift. In reality both my parents were economical. However, if something was acquired it had to be of the best quality, and in particular they were very generous with regard to the education of their children. My parents were married in the year 1874. They had met in Hanau, where my father had been known as the handsome Austrian. My mother, Sophie Hamburger, was the youngest of five brothers and sisters (Louis, Friedericke, Heinrich, Emma and Sophie). Sophie was her father's favourite and she also loved him very much. When grandfather, to compensate for his sedentary occupation, got up at five o'clock to chop wood in the courtyard of his house, Sophie also got up and made him a good cup of coffee. Afterwards he used to go to the market in Hanau and, for example, purchase a fresh carp. That was all very well, but that he went out in his flowery dressing gown was not appreciated by the daughters of a 'Justizrat'! Although I did not know my grandparents on either side, as they died before I was born in 1892, I remember very well the grandparents' house in Hanau. When I was still small I sometimes went to Hanau with my mother in order to visit the old house and the grave of my grandparents. At the level of the first floor a wooden balcony went right around the house, and it must have been pleasant to sit there in summer. In accordance with old Jewish custom we would leave two little stones on the grave. In the grave were grandmother Röschen, *née* Dilsheim, with her husband Julius Hamburger, 'the Justizrat'. Grandmother was proud of her husband's title and had it engraved on the gravestone.

 The Hamburger grandparents were both thirty-two when they married and had known each other from early youth, but had waited until grandfather earned enough as a solicitor to support a family. However, they had five healthy children. Aunt Friedericke died young and I never knew her; Uncle Louis lived in Frankfurt and both he and Uncle Adolf Hess—who married Aunt Emma—were numismaticians. Both had a good business in coins and became well-to-do, but later they quarrelled and broke off all connections. Uncle Louis married a Parisian Jewess, Aunt Emilie, who did not fit into the Klieneberger family. I was never at ease in their large house in the Mainzerlandstrasse but enjoyed cycling with my uncle, accompanied by his two dachshounds, on Sunday morning punctually at half-past six. I had a brand-new bicycle and our goal was Isenburg in the middle of the Frankfurt Stadtwald. There we breakfasted in the restaurant, Uncle on three eggs and ham and I on one boiled egg and a large glass of milk. At that time I was 11 years old and fond of all

Forebears, Home and Youth

sport such as cycling, swimming, skating. My mother's second brother, Uncle Heinrich, had married an English Jewess, Aunt Carrie. When I was four, we visited them in Nottingham, where I was sent to an English kindergarten and generally spoiled there. The most interesting of my uncles was Uncle Adolf, Aunt Emma's husband. He was very interested in art and music and, as an early admirer of Wagner, visited the Bayreuth festivals regularly with my aunt and in later life wintered in Italy. From there they always sent me a lovely box of tangerines, which arrived on my birthday and which Paula and I had to collect from the post office; to this day I remember their lovely fragrance. Uncle Adolf had a fine collection of antique wood carvings and in his study an old Italian picture of the entombment of Christ. When he was in an expansive mood he talked about Italy and would take these carvings one by one from the showcase and explain all about them and how he acquired them. I listened with great interest. This uncle was also a socialist and a freethinker. Of the children and grandchildren of my uncles and aunts there is not much to relate. Some died and the Klienebergers lost contact with the others. My memories of them were faint and have become fainter.

Now I must speak of my mother. She was an extraordinary woman and if each of her children (Carl, Otto, Anna, Emma) inherited only some of her good points they could be pleased with themselves. As a young girl she was small and delicate with fine, bright dark-brown eyes and abundant black hair. She combined great kindness with intelligence and great willpower and energy. Yet she had a gay and vivacious temperament. She lived for her family but also took great interest in her contemporaries and her younger friends. Right up to old age she was loved and admired by many. She was the leading power of the family and also 'der ruhende Pol in der Erscheinungen Flucht'.

If I had a particular wish I asked father first for permission. He answered: "Ask your mother." However, mother would say: "I have to discuss this with your father." But I knew for certain that mother was the deciding personality. Undoubtedly she had great influence on her children and we could discuss our problems with her. She only wanted sons because she thought they could get a better education, and consequently a better life than girls. She herself was very gifted but had no opportunity of developing her talents. When, then, she had two daughters as well as two sons, all of whom she loved, she insisted that equal sums of money be put aside for the education of each. She had a very modern outlook for her time and took equal pleasure in her daughters' studies and her sons' and often she said to me: "If you marry it's all right; if you don't marry it's still all right." If an examination had been successful and the result was brought home a jolly 'war dance' took place. She embraced her child and we danced around the big dining room table with exuberant gaiety. On the other hand she was not 'modern' in her moral outlook. If one of her daughters had had an affair with a man, she would have disapproved strongly and the daughter would have been turned out of the house. She had no reason to fear for her daughters in this respect. Yet she was always ready to extend generous hospitality to my friends of both sexes.

At the age of twenty-one I was a student at Göttingen University and rented a sitting-room and small bedroom (*Stube und Kammer*) from a working class family. I was quite free in my movements and the relationships with my friends of both sexes, yet it would never have occurred to me or my dear friend Paul to go beyond friendship, although we saw each other daily and he always took me home from the lectures. In any case we were so interested in our studies and enchanted by all that the university offered that I think we had no room in our hearts for flirtations. It must be remembered that we sat at the feet of David Hilbert and Carl Runge, for we both studied mathematics, though Paul was without doubt a much better mathematician than I was. But our friendship meant much to us.

After this digression I must return to the Klienebergers. I had two older brothers and an older sister. Carl was sixteen years older than I, Otto thirteen years older, and Anna (called Anny), eleven years my senior. My mother told me that when I was a baby the 11-year-old girl was run over by a carriage in the Böhmerstrasse. The neighbour shouted: "Mrs Klieneberger your Anny has been run over". Mother threw me on the bed and ran downstairs. But the child was unharmed—the horses had not touched her, nor had she been injured by the wheels! I cannot remember a time when we were all together at home, but I remember well the years when dear Anny was still with us, for I was 12 years old when she became engaged and soon afterwards got married. When I started school at six, Anny was at the teachers' training college which was housed in the same building as the Elisabethenschule (named after Goethe's mother), which I attended. This was in the Börsenplatz in Frankfurt. I used to look with pride and respect at the big girls in the teachers' training college, some of whom were my sisters friends. One old teacher, Herr Hess, knew me as Anny's little sister, and when he passed me in the corridor he usually smiled and said, "Aha,! The Klieneberger's fledgling (*Nesthäkchen*)!" My school years were happy ones. I had absolutely no ambition and unless my interest was aroused I just

Forebears, Home and Youth

dreamed. Because of this my good teacher, Herr Kolbe, used to call me "Emmy with the veil around her". He had funny, but very appropriate descriptions for us. One girl he called "Little Wilhelmina in the green clover", as she used to duck her head like a little rabbit when she couldn't answer a question. When something suddenly fell to the floor with a crash, he used to shout, "Lie down with it!" I often wondered what would have happened if a child had obeyed his order, but it never happened. I used to like writing essays and I suppose they were not too bad, but I would really wake up when we had mathematics, physics and chemistry lessons. Old Professor Kinkelin, who had already taught my very gifted sister, would put his hand on my head when I gave a good answer; this delighted me. In the upper forms we had very good teachers with modern ideas about teaching; they stimulated us greatly. We learned with great enthusiasm long scenes from plays by Schiller and Shakespeare (in English) by heart which we performed in front of the class and the teacher. I am often surprised that we hear today so many programmes on the modern media which deal with proposals for changing teaching methods and teaching material. Teachers are born! It is my opinion that nothing can make a good teacher out of a human being who has not the gift, the love and the necessary imagination for this vocation, as well as the understanding of a child's mind.

Like my sister, from the Elisabethenschule I went to the teachers' training college where the language classes were especially good, as was the instruction in mathematics and science. Our beloved teacher, Herr Rühle, who had never visited a university, knew surely as much as any college-trained person and, on top of that, he was a 'born' teacher. Yet he was later given the sack because he had not the necessary diplomas for a post in a teachers' training college. He became head of a 'Volksschule'. However his lessons had been excellent. They stimulated us (i.e. my good friend Minna Lang and me) greatly.

While still at school I read a lot of natural science such as the then much-read books by Bölsche, so that even at the age of 13 or 14 I was 'well-informed'. We possessed the numerous volumes of Brehms *Tierleben* and it was an unending source of joy to me, almost as great as a visit to the zoological gardens and the walks through the famous greenhouses of the Palmengarten. Also, like my friend Annemarie Grossmann, I subscribed to the periodical *Kosmos*. My friendship with Annemarie lasted into old age. As children we always had animals in the house, such as a frog, lizards and a tortoise, which we looked after with great care; on the way home from school in summer we used to catch, with great skill, flies which settled on the sunny walls of the houses, without injuring them. We put them into little bottles with perforated corks, which we always carried in our pockets; the bottles fitted into a hole in the net covering of the glass cage containing the frog. One after another the flies emerged from the bottle and tempted the frog, who caught them with his sticky tongue. In the winter when flies were scarce, the frog had to learn to eat meal-worms. As frogs are only attracted by something moving and only look up, I would put him on my left hand while the meal-worm wriggled on my right hand held above. The frog's eyes looked upwards and 'snap' he jumped and had secured a meal-worm on his tongue. This big meal was sufficient for two days. I used to wander with Annemarie in the local meadows where we collected flowers which we tried to identify with the help of a simple book. My sister helped in this as she was also interested in botany. With my friend Liesel Hamburger, who was always laughing, and of whom the school director Keller said "Brown Liesel, I know her by her bell" (die braune Liesel kenn ich am Gelaut: *Wilhelm Tell*, Schiller), I went swimming and cycling. Sometimes her brother Richard came with us to the Stadtwald or on longer excursions.

I saw my brothers only in their holidays when they were students and young hospital doctors. When they were expected my mother went cheerfully through the flat and said "The boys are coming". Then there was the smell of cakes and a good roast and in the kitchen a wonderful 'Polish salad' was prepared in which, besides potatoes, were bacon, herring, beetroot, onion, oil, vinegar and cream. The brothers spoiled me; Otto sang student songs to me, such as 'Im schwarzen Walfisch zu Askalon sass einst ein Mann drei Tag, bis dass er steif wie ein Besenstiel am Mamortische lag'*. I enjoyed that and took it literally in my childish imagination. Carl, the elder called me 'the little toad' (*die kleine Krott*) and liked teasing me very much. It was always pleasant when the brothers were at home in the holidays. But often I was sent on some errand or had to telephone for them in the nearby dairy, which I did reluctantly. One episode is still vivid in my memory: my brother Carl worked for a time at the Paul Ehrlich Institute in Frankfurt and one Christmas, as a surprise, he put a large wooden box for me on the gift table. I opened it and in it was a little live guinea-pig. I was delighted. In the evening the men smoked a great deal in the Christmas room, and mother, in her enthusiasm for fresh air, had opened wide the big window. It was a cold

---

* 'Once a man was staying for three days in the Black Whale pub at Ascalon until he was lying stiff like a broom-stick at the marble table.'

night and the next morning I found the guinea-pig at the open window where it had obviously spent the whole night. I was very concerned about the little animal. So Carl proposed we take it back to its siblings. We drove to the Paul-Ehrlich-Strasse and I saw for the first time the laboratory animals, rabbits, guinea-pigs, rats and mice which were kept and bred there in the basement.

Despite the many pleasures which came from being together with my older brothers and sister, it hurt me when the whole family went to the theatre or the excellent Frankfurt opera without me. The visit to the opera also occurred when my parents celebrated their silver wedding and I was only seven years old. My older brothers and sister seemed to me very gifted, clever and full of interests. Their friends came to visit us and I was just the little girl who could not share their conversation. I felt very stupid and when I read in a book by the Swiss author Spyri about the 'Block-head Trine' (*die vernagelte Trine*), for whom I felt very sorry, I compared myself to her. As I was clever with my hands and at school excelled in handicrafts and moreover was passionately fond of sewing dolls' dresses, I made up my mind to be a dressmaker, because I was not clever enough for anything else. At a very early age I was convinced by my mother's viewpoint that everyone (girl or boy) had to have a profession by which to earn their own bread. If I had not had such a good and wise mother, who had so much understanding for her youngest child, I could easily have developed a permanent inferiority complex. My sister also understood me very well, took an interest in me and taught me the names of plants and flowers on excursions or in the holidays. When, at 21, she spent a year in Paris to learn the language and take lessons in painting, she corresponded with me and sent me a few French books, of which the then much-read *L'Auberge de l'Ange Gardien* made a great impression on me. Also my brother Carl wrote to me when I was 14 and I went to him with all my problems and in a charming way he considered carefully all that the 'Krott' wrote to him. Brother Otto had a poetic bent and composed comic speeches in verse, which the little sister had to present on festive occasions in the family circle. In fact we all made verses for the entertainment and amusement of the family. For me the most enjoyable family festivals were mother's and father's birthdays. On mother's birthday, early before seven o'clock, I went with Papa into his fine, well-tended rose garden, which encircled the house. The roses were in full bloom on the 19th of June, the month of roses; we cut enough of the beautiful blooms to fill several vases. In the afternoon friends and relations came to express birthday wishes and for coffee and birthday cake. We were snowed under with asparagus, strawberries and flowers—I found that it was wonderful!

My father had a special love for flowers and a general interest in nature. During the winter we always had the most beautiful hyacinths between the double windows, and if the inside window was opened the most heavenly scent came into the room. On the 1st of May he always took me at five o'clock in the morning to the Stadtwald, where after a walk through the fresh spring wood we would go into one of the popular restaurants such as the Forsthaus. Also on Sunday afternoons we regularly went walking either to the Forsthaus or round the 'Ringstrasse', a popular Frankfurt walk. This bored me very much because it was always repeated and no other children came along. As a result it was always my great wish that it would rain cats and dogs on Sunday afternoons, a wish which sometimes came true.

When I was 12 years old my sister became engaged to her Latin teacher. In fact after some years of teaching she still wanted to obtain a university training and prepared herself for the university entrance examination. But her engagement put a stop to that. When she told me about this I was so unhappy that I cried the whole afternoon. Oberlehrer Dr Julius Schönemann, who was nearly thirty years older than I and for whom I had great respect, came into our family and took my sister away. He was a good man with great knowledge and ambition but I also saw him as a pedantic person; yet I shall never forget how, with great kindness and sympathy, when I had been dismissed from my post in 1933, he went all over Frankfurt with me, from pillar to post, so to speak; in particular we visited all the Jewish lawyers we knew to find out what could be done! But, of course there was nothing to be done! He was then 70 years old and with his 'anima candida' and as a true German (he was not a Jew) he understood much less than we Jews what was happening, and it cut him more deeply because it was directed against his beloved and revered wife. Anyhow, in those days we did not know, as we do now, all that can be done by and through human beings to their fellow men.

The mention of my good brother-in-law made me digress. I was just 12 years old when my sister was engaged and that summer we, my mother, myself and the engaged couple went for an unforgettably impressive journey to Switzerland. We spent the summer holidays in Hilterfingen on the Thuner See. I had already been taken to Switzerland a few times as a small child, but then I could not yet appreciate the beauty of nature. But now that my eyes were opened, I was enchanted by the beautiful lake surrounded by mountains. A night ascent of the Niesen, where we saw

Forebears, Home and Youth

the sun rise, made a lasting impression on me. My mother, then 56, was still a brilliant and enthusiastic mountaineer. Also swimming in and rowing on the lake were wonderful pastimes. I still admire the courage of my mother, who could not swim, yet entrusted herself to me to go rowing on the lake. Also at that time I first saw the glacier garden at Lucerne and the Lion carved in the rock by Thorwaldsen, all unforgettable experiences.

My brothers were not only good to me when I was a child but also when I was a young woman. My brother Otto invited me on a trip on the Rhine and also to Würzburg where I saw quite a bit of my second cousin Edith, and met her fiancé, the mathematician Otto Haupt (later Professor in Erlangen). Edith had been brought up by her grandmother Oppenheimer, the favourite cousin of my mother, and her daughter, Aunt Clara. Clara Oppenheimer was one of the first women to study medicine in Germany and she had practised in Würzburg. I was very much at home in the Oppenheimer house and Edith was a dear cousin to me. In the Nazi period and in the following war time we were completely out of touch; but afterwards we renewed our correspondence and in the year 1969 we met each other, as well as a mutual Swiss cousin, Dr Sigwart Frank, in Zürich. We four old people experienced a few charming days together in great harmony.

My brother Carl also travelled with me; we both liked walking. Carl's wife Gustel whom I loved like a sister, was not able to climb because of heart trouble. So I met Carl in Vienna where I arrived at 7 o'clock in the morning after a sleepless night on a third class wooden seat—but after a good breakfast, a thorough sight-seeing tour was organized by my systematic brother. This went on until late afternoon, when I fell asleep on a bench in the park. We saw all the famous places in Vienna; of course we also went to nearby attractions such as the Kobenzl and the Wiener Wald; as well as Grinzing 'beim Heurigen'. From Vienna we went to Zell am See; there we swam and walked a great deal. Twice we climbed the Schmittenhöhe. We made other excursions, but I could not understand why my good brother, wearing holiday clothes, never wished to sit on the grass for a rest. The 'Professor' was also a little pedantic. In another summer the 'frische Nehrung' was chosen for a holiday. We crossed it from one end to the other; the walking days spent there were equally pleasant.

I cannot talk about my parents' house and the Klienebergers without mentioning Paula. She was one of the most important people in the household. She came to us, 19 years old, a poor simple village girl from

Poppenweiler near Ludwigsburg. She had already been in two families as a maid before she came to us. There she had been badly treated and had not even been given enough to eat. She was slim, had beautiful dark eyes, and yet I wonder if one could have called her a beauty. I was five years old when she came to us, and I can still well remember how Mother, on that first afternoon, sent me out with her to show her the shops where we made our purchases. So I showed her the greengrocer's opposite, which had belonged to the somewhat faded 'Frau Belz' (*belzig*, shrivelled), who then was made into 'Frau Schmelz' by the fresh-looking younger second husband. Then we went to the dairy and to one of the grocers' shops of Schade und Füllgrabe, which were found throughout the suburbs of Frankfurt. Finally we went to the excellent butcher's shop of Krapp's. They had an only son who was a little older than I, who later went into the business and used to bring the meat we ordered and take orders for the next day. He was such a handsome young lad with blond hair and blue eyes and good manners. When, some time after the Second World War I went once again to Frankfurt to visit my dear sister-in-law Gustel, who also used to buy her meat at Krapp's, I saw him again as a hobbling old man, sad that his only son did not want to take over the business. How good was the ham and macaroni dish which my mother or Paula used to prepare from the 'ham scraps' from Herr Krapp. It was not really scraps but cuts from the sides of the large hams. And then the splendid Krapp sausages which we had at home with savoy cabbage!

Paula was our factotum for 20 years. She cleaned, washed and cooked, and always looked nice—in the morning with a coloured apron and freshly changed in the afternoon with a white apron. She came to life with us, and mother was very good to her. She had lupus on one ear; my brother Carl, who at that time was an assistant doctor at the Heiliggeist Hospital in Frankfurt, took an interest in her complaint. The ear was operated on, she underwent a long treatment and finally was cured. She learned to arrange her hair so skilfully that no one noticed the missing ear lobe. I spent a lot of time with her in the kitchen, sat on what we called the sideboard, dangling my legs, and told her all that had happened at school. I was allowed to grind the coffee, clean the knives (they were not rustless in those days), top and tail the red currants for jam-making, and help in drying up. But I was never allowed to try my hand at cooking. She said "You only make the pots dirty and I have to wash them again". And so I was always put off! Mother allowed Paula to go swimming with me, she bought her skates and a subscription to the rink in the Palmengarten and so we went out happily together skating on winter afternoons. I practised with great eagerness on the rink, learned curves and figures of eight and was quite enthusiastic when the band played and we could skim over the ice in time to the music. The skill achieved at that time stood me in great stead later when I was a bacteriologist at the Frankfurt Hygiene Institute. For my respected Chief was a very good skater and sometimes on fine winter days we went during the lunch hour to the nearby rink. A sandwich was enough for lunch and I had the satisfaction of gliding over the ice partnered by my Chief. He said later to his secretary "Die Doktorin cuts a good figure on the ice", which remark got back to me.

Paula was clever and had a considerable thirst for knowledge. Although she came from a village school her spelling was faultless. She asked for 'classical works' as Christmas presents and so made the acquaintance of German literature by her own efforts. It was delightful to be in her spotless kitchen on winter afternoons. The fire crackled in the kitchen range, Paula was neatly dressed and sat at the table and practised round-hand writing from examples, because her own handwriting no longer satisfied her. When she had been with us for twenty years she married an engineer from Linz in Austria, who had literally courted her for the 'seven years'. He knew her value very well; the wedding was at our house. Unfortunately he died after ten years of happy married life and she returned to her village home. From the letters she wrote to me I learned that she had enough to live on comfortably, looked after the neighbours' children and did much good for her friends in the village and for her relations. Long after the Second World War I met her in Stuttgart where we spent two delightful days together. We visited the 'Wilhelma', a mixed botanical and zoological garden. At the conclusion of our tour she said, "I think we have seen everything and you can explain it all so well". She lived to be over 80 and often wrote to me. All the letters started, "Dear, dear Emmy". She identified herself completely with our family; she spoke of our house, our garden, our lovely Christmases. When I last saw her, she was a charming old lady with fine features, dressed well and tastefully all in black.

I want now to write a little about the town of Frankfurt, in which I was born and brought up. The once so beautiful town on the river Main is connected with Sachsenhausen, on the opposite bank, by several bridges. As our local poet Friedrich Stoltze said, from 'Dribbderbach', the beautiful skyline of the old commercial town presented itself at its best. Outstanding among its towers were the old Saalhof, Leonard's church and the tower of the old Gothic cathedral looming over all. Of the bridges, the 'Eiserne Steg' and the 'Alte Brücke' with its Norman arches were regarded as specially beautiful characteristics of the old town. Sometimes on a school holiday I went with Annemarie to the 'Maininsel' which was reached by steps from the 'Old Bridge'. We had sketch books with us and tried to capture some of the detail of the beautiful panorama. Annemarie succeeded quite well, I less so, but we both enjoyed it. When we had visitors we always went with them through the old part of the town, visited the Römerberg and the Römer itself, where the 'Roman Emperors of the German Nation' (*die römischen Kaiser deutscher Nation*) once were crowned. We ascended the wide staircase to the 'Römersaal', where the pictures of the emperors hang. The charming old courtyard of the Römer, das 'Römerhöfchen' was on show and we enjoyed seeing the old patrician houses grouped around the Römerberg. We told our visitors about the Fountain of Justice in the middle of the square, from which red and white wine flowed on the occasion of a coronation, at which time a whole oxen would be roasted on a spit on the Römerberg. Also very beautiful were the gardens laid out where the fortifications of the Middle Ages used to stand; they surrounded the whole inner town.

In Sachsenhausen is one of the gems of the city, the Städel picture gallery, in which were to be found pictures by almost all the great masters. The Senckenberg Museum with its palaeological collection and its library were justifiably famous and stimulated visits. Frankfurt was in my youth a centre of intellectual activity; exhibitions of famous painters could be seen in the halls of the Neue Mainzerstrasse. There were the 'Museum concerts' on Friday evenings, which were repeated on Sunday mornings. The famous conductor Mengelberg came from Amsterdam to conduct them. The Friday evening concerts were attended by the 'haute volée'; the same concerts on Sunday mornings rather by the educated middle class. When I was employed at the Hygiene Institute I had a season ticket to the Sunday concerts for many years. In the twenties, together with the wife of my esteemed Professor, Dr Martin Möbius, I had a monthly subscription to the opera, which gave us both much pleasure, and I particularly remember, among other performances, those of *Aïda* and the *Mikado*.

Frankfurt was, of course, also the birthplace of Goethe, and the Goethe-House where he was born and brought up, was therefore a frequently visited and famous place. In the poet's wonderful book *Dichtung und Wahrheit* much can be read about the beautiful town and its history. In my youth Frankfurt was a so-called 'Judenstadt' (Jewish town), as a wide stratum of the middle class consisted of Jewish families. In the High

Forebears, Home and Youth

School for girls, administered by the Town Authorities, half the children in my form were Jewish. Therefore I hardly noticed any anti-Semitism at school. Nevertheless, as I learned from a few personal experiences, it did exist. In the first few years in my form at school the girls, or rather their mothers, sometimes gave afternoon parties to which they invited their friends by distributing little letter cards among them. It struck me that some Christian children only invited Christians and some Jewish girls only Jewish children. I myself had friends in each camp and in any case it did not bother me. A second experience shocked me. In summer I used to go almost every day to swim in the swimming bath on the river Main. Frequently girls I knew were also there. One afternoon I noticed some of them whispering together and as I came out of my bathing cabin, after my swim, in a beautiful white sailor dress, they threw at me pieces of slimy green algae from the edge of the swimming pool, soiling me from head to foot. I was completely dumbfounded and went sadly home. At the time in my childish innocence I could not understand this incident. But later its significance became clear to me. Only much later, at the university, did I come up against anti-Semitism again. A medical student in his final year, a handsome young man from North Germany paid me some attention and several times asked me to go for a walk with him. In Göttingen there was the nice custom that the girl bought cakes at the baker's and the young man paid for the coffee and service, because there was nothing to be had in the little restaurants in the woods except coffee and plates, etc. And how good the Streuselkuchen and the Bienenstich were at Göttingen! One day this young man was no longer interested in me. When I met him in the street, for you could not avoid meeting in this small university town, and I asked him why I never saw him now; he replied that he had too much work to do for his examinations. I knew instinctively the true state of affairs and told myself that such a man was not worth my attention.

Yet again I had a much more serious conflict with an anti-Semitic professor of mathematics. It was shortly before the State Examination which was called at that time 'pro facultate docendi' and which entitled one to teach senior classes at high school, 'Gymnasiums' and 'Teachers' Training Colleges'. I had already obtained my doctorate in 1917 in botany with zoology and mathematics as subsidiary subjects. A supplementary brief examination in philosophy was obligatory. The work for my doctorate was accepted for my thesis in biology and I had to submit a written mathematical paper. In a preceding mathematical seminar I had been asked to discuss non-Euclidean geometry on a spherical surface. The principal of the seminar, Professor Bieberbach, who apparently at the time was satisfied with my little lecture, gave me the same theme for my examination thesis. I worked assiduously for some months, read the relevant literature and finally set down the results of these activities. I did not expect a brilliant mark for this, since gradually I had become more and more interested in biology. Yet I thought I had at least deserved a 'satisfactory' grading. So I was astonished when the Professor summoned me to him and showed me that he had marked the paper as 'unsatisfactory' and what especially disgusted me, he had written scornful and indecent comments in the margins such as 'Bockmist'! I also knew that the paper would be circulated among my other examiners. At our interview this professor now began to overwhelm me with reproaches, saying among other things, that I seemed to think that results could be achieved without any work on my part. I was filled with indignation and told him he could describe my work as bad but he had no right to attack my integrity and without waiting for an answer or looking back I left the room. Professor Möbius, who over the years had become my fatherly friend and advisor, said, "If he wants to fail you in the oral examination he can easily do so even if you are well prepared". From that moment I didn't do a stroke of work in mathematics, but concentrated on the other subjects. Because if I failed in one subject only, I could take it again after another semester, and if I wished, under another Professor. It would be said that I passed but for one subject. I was prepared for this failure. Then the day of the examination arrived. In botany and zoology I passed with distinction, philosophy was 'very good'. Then came mathematics for which I had made no preparations. I no longer remember the questions and answers of this painful session; it seems to me now that my only answer was, "Don't know". Nevertheless in view of my other marks and the satisfaction expressed by the other professors with my work, the mathematics professor must have had an attack of cowardice, for he wrote a large 'satisfactory' in the examination record and so I passed the whole examination. At the time it did not occur to me that the behaviour of this professor was caused by anti-Semitism, though I knew that he had done me an injustice, but later at the time of the Nazi regime I learned that he had shown himself to be very anti-Semitic and that he acted ruthlessly and shamelessly against his Jewish colleagues. His speeches and written articles caused much indignation in England at that time (see: *Nature*, 18th August 1934, Letter to the editor by G.H. Hardy, New College Oxford). However, after the lapse of so many years and with a more objective and quieter mind I am inclined to believe the judgement of *old* present-day German mathematicians, whose opinion is that this professor was not in his right mind. This seems to me a very plausible explanation for his quite illogical behaviour in my case and for his articles which a present day reader could only term as 'quite mad'.

Racism is still a very controversial theme, though today it is particularly the colour of the skin that causes discrimination and injustice. Yet anti-Semitism has also not died out. However, it has never hurt me personally. I was proud of my descent and of my family, although the attitude taken by many German Jews displeased me. In general they were very nationalistic; many of them wished to be considered first as Germans and wanted to forego Judaism. Many of them changed their names; they were baptized. In my youth no Jewish scholar could count on obtaining a university chair unless he was baptized. Of course, before the First World War a few drops of 'holy' water sufficed. In the period between the revolution of 1919 and the coming of the Nazi party even this was no longer necessary. Even my revered and beloved Chief, Professor Max Neisser, had paid this tribute in his youth, although he had married into one of the most 'aristocratic' and leading Jewish families of Frankfurt, the Hallgartens. But should he have allowed his great talent for organization to be wasted because of this 'trifle' and bureaucratic stupidity? As he himself said, at the celebration of his sixtieth birthday, he had three real children and three intellectual offspring. These latter were the Institute of Hygiene, the Central Library of the Municipal Hospitals and the Tuberculosis Welfare Organization, all of which had been initiated by him. The Mendelssohn family is a good and noteworthy example of this attitude of one group of German Jews. For whereas Moses Mendelssohn, whom Lessing has immortalized in *Nathan der Weise*, wandered into Berlin through 'the Jew's gate' as a poor young lad, lean and hunchbacked, and observed the old customs throughout his life, his well-to-do son, Abraham Mendelssohn already had his four children baptized (see: Sebastian Hensel, *Die Familie Mendelssohn*). Felix, who took his Christian status seriously, composed music for the church with the same enthusiasm as he composed secular music, and added Bartholdy to his name on the example of his uncle who lived in Rome. Fanny and Rebekka, his gifted sisters, married Christians, Fanny the painter Hensel, Rebekka the well-known mathematician Lejeune-Dirichlet, who was the successor in Göttingen to the famous physicist and mathematician Gauss. One could easily quote examples of less famous German Jews. For example we used to recount that the bacteriologist known in the literature as Conradi had the 'Radi' cut off from his name in Munich. (To understand this one must realize that the Munich beer-drinkers used to eat a radish—*Radi*—with their beer.)

My own family belonged to that same category of Jews who tried to be assimilated. In my youth this seemed wrong to me; today I can understand this better, although under Hitler it could be seen that we had backed the wrong horse, for it made emigration more difficult for some and it was quite impossible for the baptized families to go to Palestine, as it was then called. My parents were not baptized but they withdrew from the Jewish religious community and called themselves 'free-thinkers' (*freireligiös*). My brothers were so compelled by the desire to divest themselves of Jewishness that they got themselves baptized and joined the 'Student Corps' which excluded Jews, at the university. They sometimes came home after a duelling session with heads bound up and reeking of carbolic. My brothers were good doctors, industrious and ambitious in the best sense of the word and they wished to get on in their profession. It was understood that the 'senior members' of the corps would use their influence to help younger members in their applications for posts. I don't know whether my brothers were ever helped in their careers by their connections with their corps—whatever the case may have been I personally found these student corps distasteful. The duelling and exchange of 'cuts' (*Schmisse*) seemed to me ridiculous, and when in Göttingen I saw these student corps returning to the city on horse-drawn carts, tipsy and bawling after their customary drinking parties, it revolted me.

But as for baptism, apart from true religious conversions, there are two schools of thought, both plausible. One school is of the opinion that a man should not leave the circle into which he is born. Rather a man ought to be proud of his descent, of the customs and usages of his ancestors and if that does not suit the other people one should not bother about it. In my youth I inclined to this opinion, which was contrary to that of my family. The other school of thought was all for assimilation. If a man has settled down among another people should he not accept their customs and usages which in the end may include acceptance of their beliefs? In the first case one is cut off and becomes disliked; in the second case it is possible that one is accepted in the new circle and then assimilation takes place. In fact if one opts for the second point of view the motives are only partly idealistic; they are to some extent dictated by the hope of personal advantage. And if the advantages were not wanted for oneself they were wanted for one's children. This was probably the case with the Mendelssohns, and so it was also with my family. My sister Anny was persuaded by the family, especially her brothers to be baptized; she was only 18 years old and still training as a teacher; the little sister Emmy, 7 years old, followed suit. This was therefore my position when I grew up. What would I have decided for myself? I don't know! Was it an advantage for me? I think not. In any case when I applied for a post at the Frankfurt Institute for Hygiene it was no longer important since under the government of the Weimar Republic the question about denomination was not included. This lasted only a short time, until Hitler came to power. Then it suddenly became a question of descent and not of religion. And those who had pinned their hopes on assimilation had made the wrong choice. In England conditions were quite different; for there the denomination is and was insignificant when personnel for the filling of posts is chosen. Today with the considerable number of coloured immigrants which have taken up residence in England the problem of assimilation looms greater than ever before. However, in my old age my decided opinion is that assimilation should be promoted as much and as rapidly as possible for segregation is always offensive and produces bad feelings on both sides. For the coloured immigrants the paramount step is the learning of the new language. This applies naturally to all kinds of immigrants, who often do not realize how much annoyance they cause if they speak the language of their hosts in a broken manner.

There are two different kinds of anti-Semitism. One is a quite general prejudice against all Jews; the other and in my experience more widespread kind, makes exceptions. With this latter attitude Jews are generally disliked, but when an individual is met and liked, the fact that he or she is a Jew is completely forgotten. Another aspect of anti-Semitism which is widespread also makes exceptions, but in the opposite way. If one meets a disagreeable Jew he or she is described as 'the specially unpleasant Jewish type', who is to be blamed for all the rest being despised. All these people, whether Christians or Jews, forget that as dear old Paula said, "Our Lord has all kinds of customers", and that there is a variety of types in all races and peoples. The origin of anti-Semitism has certainly been frequently investigated and discussed; there are however many other anti-isms. I am here only interested in the form in which I met it. But I am convinced that its continued existence is furthered by childrens' parents, by the people surrounding them, possibly by their teachers, all of them influencing them at an early age. The child's mind is credulous and very receptive and retains its impressions like a soft piece of metal, which then becomes hard and keeps its shape for all time. The National Socialists knew this better than anyone else and made one hundred per cent use of it. In this connection I remember a story which I read many years ago in the book of an Alsace minister about the Franco-German war of 1870: a child came running home and called to his mother, "I've seen the French soldiers, and what do you think, they are not devils but just people like us!"

Following my baptism at seven, in my first year at school I had religious instruction with the Jewish children, in the second year and subsequent ones with the Christian children of my class. I don't know what is intended by starting religious instruction with such young children. I assume and think I remember that we were told selected stories from the Bible. In the middle school we became acquainted with dogma. We had an unintelligent teacher in religious instruction and the same one in arithmetic. I could not grasp the dogmatic teaching and sometimes—with complete innocence—put a question which obviously annoyed this teacher since he could not answer it and took it as a personal attack. I received bad marks from him in religion and in arithmetic. I found this unjust, without worrying about it; there were so many interesting things to do. Sport and handicraft such as sewing, knitting and crocheting gave me great pleasure at this time of my life. My good mother saw to it that I did my homework, but whether I came home with a 'good' or only a 'satisfactory' she saw no reason to scold me.

In the upper classes all this changed; arithmetic and mathematics were given by Herr Rühle, who gave us excellent instruction and who also taught us in the Teachers' Training College in all the natural sciences and in mathematics, as I mentioned earlier on. We liked these lessons very much, that is my dear friend Minna Lang, whom I met in the college, and I. In the upper classes of the Elisabethenschule religious instruction was given by 'old Fritz' (Professor Fritz Rehorn) a greatly beloved teacher, who, although very near retirement, greatly stimulated our interest. He read various sorts of works with us, for example Martin Luther's *On the Freedom of a Christian* (*Von der Freiheit eines Christenmenschen*). Especially stimulating and interesting though were the confirmation lessons of Pfarrer Dr Erich Förster, who was engaged by our reformed community. He was very liberal and a number of 'baptized Jews' were in his parish. It was told that he was alleged to have said, "I love my Jews, they are so charitable". He was a fine, wise man who had children from the Volksschule and High Schools in his confirmation classes and had something to give to all. He helped us, especially me, over our doubts about dogma, in that, for example, he presented the confirmation to us as nothing more than an ancient custom. I held him in great esteem and for many years after confirmation I still went to his sermons in the reformed church. In those young years I went through a phase when I was rather religious. But I no longer took communion after confirmation; the symbolic drinking of the wine and taking the Host seemed to me completely 'pagan'. My mother was very honest to me; she said, "I don't believe anything, but it certainly would be very good for you if you could". But in later life I have never been convinced that men draw strength from the belief in any particular religion or from Christianity as taught at school or in the churches. A belief in the sense of life and its goodness in spite of all the evil of this world is necessary. Such a belief that gives strength of character and a continuous stimulus to try our best comes from the innermost depth of the being. My own church- and school-taught religion withered completely in the course of the years. I saw how much injustice had been done in the name of religion, in the name of Christianity of one form or the other, and is still perpetrated. All peoples have invented formal religions and today still form themselves into societies, who announce supernatural happenings and are not satisfied with the idea that we are born, live and die like the grass and the flowers in the fields, for living and dying are connected with each other; and I firmly believe that we must try to live as good a life as possible, because if not many people tried to do this, our world would be an even sadder place than it is now.

In spite of all I said previously, I am of the opinion that free religious teaching should be a school subject. The reading and studying of the Bible is of paramount importance for young people and is a great asset in later life. For the Bible is one of the most interesting and enlightening books. It is full of wisdom, beauty and poetry. How beautiful are the psalms and how full of wisdom the similes!

The fate of the Jews all over the world moves me greatly. I hope that in the course of time a solution of their problems will eventually come to pass.

Here I should like to add something in respect of Zionism. When I read the wonderful autobiography (*Trial and Error*) by Dr Chaim Weizmann, who became the first President of Israel in 1948, I could fully understand that the oppressed Jews in many lands and particularly in Russia regarded Palestine as their 'Promised Land'. The pogroms and the humiliating and degrading conditions under which these Jews lived through the centuries have forcefully driven men like Dr Weizmann to believe that Zionism and Palestine was their only salvation. They emigrated to Palestine in great flocks, particularly when Hitler came into power, and they changed with the greatest enthusiasm and with much sacrifice the difficult, neglected and arid land into the beautiful country which is now their homeland, 'Israel'. These people deserve our highest admiration. On the other hand many Jews have assimilated themselves into the society of their host countries and regarded themselves as citizens of their European fatherland, in which they were born and reared. I have already mentioned the Mendelssohns. When father Abraham asked his son Felix in which country he would like to work he answered, "Only in Germany". He certainly regarded it as his fatherland.

When in 1911 I passed the examination for school teachers at the age of 19, the question arose whether I should apply in Frankfurt to teach in the girls' schools. I found that I knew very little. How could I teach school children with such slight knowledge, with so many gaps in it? I was also shy and had little self-confidence. I asked my parents if they would allow me to go to university. The good people agreed. By the standards of that time they were not really well-to-do. They lived simply and modestly but had no financial worries. Father was approaching 80, Mother 63. They still had to keep me for some years and pay for my studies. But I had first to pass the 'Abitur'. So I took Latin lessons with a Primaner (sixth-former) from the Lessing Gymnasium and mathematics with Professor Mannheimer, the much-liked teacher at the only Gymnasium for girls in Frankfurt, the Schillerschule. The Latin lessons were supervised by brother-in-law Julius. The mathematics lessons consisted in my working from a book at home and Professor Mannheimer looking through my homework. In autumn 1912 I entered the Unterprima of the Schillerschule. Most of my school class-mates were not much younger than I because at that time there were not many girls who wanted to go to university, and most of them lost a year or two in passing from the girls' school to the Gymnasium. All went quite well for me at the Schiller school except for the little skirmishes which I had with Dr Bojunga, the Director, who took the German lessons. He was extremely nationalistic, not in the sense of the later Nazis, but rather like the right-wing party in Germany. He wanted to eliminate all foreign words from our language; we should replace the word 'Ideal' by 'Hochziel'. I found this absurd since foreign words to some extent enrich the language. I stood out against this. I also once quoted Horace in a German essay. We were then reading his odes in the Latin class. He wrote in red ink in the margin, "It would be better for a German girl, in a German school, in a German town, to use the

German language", and then came an equivalent German quotation. Once we were supposed to write an essay based on a line from one of the choruses in 'The Bride from Messina' which says, "But war too has its honour". I liked the choruses from 'The Bride from Messina' (Schiller) but not the theme of the essay. I wrote a pacifist essay and described vividly the horror and devastation of war, only at the end I conceded that a nation attacked has to defend itself. The Director judged my viewpoint rather than my essay and marked it 'unsatisfactory'. So I spoiled my report in German. But in the Abitur my German was graded between satisfactory and good. Anyhow, I was exempted from the oral examination, on the grounds of "good class work and satisfactory written papers in the Abitur". The good Director did not really mean to be unpleasant and later treated me very well when I came to the Schillerschule as a 'probationer'.

CHAPTER II

College Years in Göttingen and Frankfurt

IN THE YEAR 1913, at the age of 21, I chose Göttingen as my first university town because mathematics and sciences flourished there, and also because my brother Otto then had a post as registrar at the psychiatric clinic of the university. I had been bored in my last year at the Schillerschule; I was already too old for the school. But at the university boredom vanished. I registered as a student at the university; at that time anyone who had passed the Abitur was accepted. There was no lack of places for students as there is today. In the registry of the university there was a list of accommodation, that is a list of recommended rooms with respectable people. I chose a living-room and a small bedroom in the 'Allee', a wide street lined with trees which led from the station to the town centre. My landlady was a fat, uneducated, rather coarse but good-natured woman who obviously had never let to a woman student before and was not quite sure what to expect. Her husband worked on the railway and they had three children. I paid a rent of 20 Marks a month, for which she also kept my rooms clean. I had to pay a little extra for the fire which she lit for me in an iron stove every day in winter. The house was old and had old-fashioned indoor sanitation; every three months a tanker drove up with a pump and a long hose to empty the cesspit in the yard; then on that one morning or afternoon one could not stay in the house because of the stink. My sitting-room had a special entrance leading into it from the staircase. But to get to the toilet I had to use my landlady's entrance which led firstly into the kitchen and then into a passage from which a door led to the room in question. Of course, there was no running water in the bedroom. But there was a basin and jug on the wash-table and a pail in the corner. The bed was good and above it was a wall-hanging on which in red cross-stitch was embroidered "While you live scatter flowers of love and save each other from heartache". This served particularly for my edification! I prepared my breakfast and evening meal myself. There were nice shops in the 'Fressgasse' (I have forgotten the real name), where one could buy, besides bread, butter by the ounce in the shape of a shell, ham, cheese and good Göttinger 'Mettwurst'. Everything catered for the students in this small university town. Lunch was taken in one of the many 'private dining rooms' which were set up in private houses like a small restaurant. For one Mark one could eat good family cooking in satisfying quantities. There I became acquainted with North German cooking, dishes such as liver with rice and apple, liver sausage with raisins and cold, sweet fruit soups. One sent one's smalls home for washing once a week and a week later it returned freshly washed and ironed. Once a week I went to the public baths for a hot bath and also had my hair washed at the hairdressers. Each month I received a cheque from my father for 120 Marks, which fully sufficed for my needs, the lecture fees and the occasional purchase of a book. From the list of lectures it was easy to select the correct ones since it stated whether they were for beginners or advanced students. Thus in the summer term of 1913, I attended the following:

   Introduction to philosophy, by Dr Reinach
   Differential and integral calculus, by Professor Runge
   Experimental physics; first part, by Professor Riecke
   Fundamentals of botany, by Professor Peters
   Plant physiology, by Professor Berthold
   Botanical microscopy course for beginners, also by Berthold

In my third term, summer 1914, I attended:

   Differential equations, by Professor Hilbert
   Practice in differential equations, by Dr Hecke
   Analytical geometry, by Dr Courant
   Practice in analytical geometry, also by Dr Courant
   Hume and the English empiricism, by Dr Reinach
   Zoology, survey of the whole field, by Professor Ehlers

Memoirs

Demonstrations in the botanical garden, by Professor Berthold
Practical work in the Physics Institute for mathematicians and
 physicists, by Professor Riecke.

In summer lectures began at 7.15 a.m. and in winter at 8.15 a.m. I still remember quite well the large iron stove which in winter during the 8-9 o'clock lecture, spread its pleasant warmth through the old-fashioned mathematics lecture room in the Allee. During the lectures we made rough notes as best as we could on a note-pad, then in the afternoon the mathematics lectures were written up in full sentences, accompanied by drawings and formulae made all 'ship-shape'. At the end of each term each separate lecture, written in paper-booklets specially sold for the purpose, was bound at the bookbinders, so that at the end one had a whole series of such volumes to put in the bookcase at home. In this way the contents of the mathematics lectures were well and truly impressed on the mind. In botany and zoology this was not necessary; there were easily comprehensible books available.

Since later in my life as a bacteriologist I was no longer concerned with mathematics, for which in my youth I cherished a secret and not completely reciprocated love, I have now completely forgotten this whole discipline. This goes so far that today I no longer know what Professor Hilbert had to say about differential equations in his lectures; but I have also completely forgotten English empiricism. But we studied with great enthusiasm in those days at Göttingen, the lectures were a great enjoyment. The practical botany and Göttingen's beautiful botanical gardens are still vivid in my memory. How often I used to go there to impress the botanical names on my memory. Naturally, we formed life-long friendships there; I have already mentioned my good and gifted friend Paul. I took part in the physics practical work with his sister Minnie. Then botany and zoology provided the first contact with 'Pussy', a parson's daughter from Lübeck. From this developed a deep friendship based on similar outlooks. We visited each other in our 'digs', and also invited other fellow students, for example to eat home-made ice cream. Göttingen was a charming little university town at the time of my college days. The whole town was surrounded by the 'Wall' laid out with gardens where once had been mediaeval fortifications. One was soon out of town, in the open country, in the woods and we had fine walks to the 'Hain' and other favoured spots for 'coffee excursions'. On Sundays we sometimes went further afield, for example to the beautifully situated Hannöverisch Münden. True, we industriously attended our lectures,

College Years

but on one fine winter day, it occurred to Pussy and me to ascend the Gaussturm with borrowed sledges and then we tobogganed down through the powdery snow. That day, on which for once we skipped all the lectures, remained long with us as a pleasant memory. On my birthday Pussy came early in the morning and set up for me on my table candles, stuck in potatoes for candle sticks. In the evening brother Otto invited both of us for a birthday dinner in the cosy Ratskeller. I was also sometimes invited with my brother by his chief, Professor Schultze. When people asked my brother at home, "How does your little sister behave in company?" he answered, "She is the quiet one in the corner, who observes everything". That probably was true, for I did not care much for parties, dances and such occasions.

We enjoyed our youth. We occupied ourselves with our studies, with other interests, including sport, our friendships and our families. We worked seriously, with the aim of a subsequent profession. We had a feeling of responsibility towards our parents and spent the money they sent us carefully and almost entirely on essentials. We never thought of buying a dress or something to wear; we were indeed well provided in this way from home. I am still moved today, when I think of my father's parting words, "And don't be too economical, if you need more write home". But the occasion never arose! So we lived at that time, but of what happened in the country, in Europe, in the world, we knew nothing. We read no newspapers, we never had political discussions, no debates about current topics. We lived in another world, in a cloud-cuckoo-land quite different from today's students and young people. True, there were occasional social gatherings with dances, sandwiches and soft drinks; we even had a society for women students, but there we never discussed affairs of the country, municipal conditions, questions of university organizations, or even womens' rights. It almost seemed as if such things as institutions of state, of the university, etc. were rigorous laws established from time immemorial and remaining thus for all eternity. The idea of upsetting them never came into our minds. Thus in the summertime of 1914 we had not the slightest inkling that in Europe, even throughout the world, war was looming over our heads. Even in my school days I used to be annoyed that in our extremely boring history lessons we learned so much about past wars and even had to learn by heart the dates of those wars. The stupid wars of olden days, I thought, how do they concern us? There can no longer be any wars in our times. It would have been better if we had been allowed to learn fewer dates but more about the causative events and told about the machinations of the politicians and the parties and business interests supporting them!

Because of all this the outbreak of war at the beginning of August 1914 fell upon us like a thunderbolt out of the blue, yes, like a sudden tornado which threatened to sweep over us. What was to happen now to us, to our country? We went through the streets of Göttingen in consternation. In the Weender Strasse my friend Minna and I met Paul and Minnie Pignol. We shook hands, we did not know what to say to each other. Eventually, we did the most natural thing: we said good-bye to our friends in great sadness, packed our trunks and travelled home. There also was complete consternation; we felt that our way of life was collapsing and knew we could never return to our old ways. And this was really the case. Anybody who tries to tell a present generation that the Germans hated the English and the English the Germans tells complete lies. There were no such feelings among ordinary people.

My brothers were called up. The young students, including my friend Paul volunteered for the army, for they were told the fatherland was in danger. My brother Otto came home from his summer holiday; he still had two days before he had to join his army unit as a military doctor. He wanted to purchase his equipment and in these two days I went around Frankfurt with him in continuous rain; I felt as if I had a temperature but did not want to think of myself at a time when my brothers and all my male acquaintances had to go to war. When I took my temperature on the day after the departure of my brother, the thermometer read 40 °C. I developed severe pleurisy which lasted for a long time. My mother nursed me untiringly and lovingly as only a mother can. In the long weeks while I lay in bed an unending stream of troops, horse-drawn guns and riders passed by my window, because at that time we no longer lived in our own house but in a ground-floor flat in the Baustrasse. I felt terribly sad; in those weeks I had plenty of time to think about the implications of the war. I realized that young men were going to the front to shoot down their opposite numbers, other young men like themselves. On both sides were men on the threshold of adult life, just beginning to experience this world, young men who had the same ideals, the same aims. Instead of killing each other they should shake hands, embrace each other and become life-long friends. I knew from my own experience how much like each other they were, those German and English youths. For not very long before 1914, in fact in the summer of 1911, I travelled to England with a group of Frankfurt pupils from high school and teachers' training college to spend a holiday in the 'Holiday Fellowship Centres'. This organization had been founded by a Mr Leonard who had had a

College Years

theological training, but later made it his life's task to promote friendship between different classes of young people and between youths of different nations. The holiday homes, which were unpretentious, were all situated in beautiful surroundings and, as Mr Leonard intended, young people from different social backgrounds met there, including also German and English people, meeting for the first time. Here also friendships were formed and, for example, I corresponded for several years with a young English girl after I spent those wonderful weeks in the Peak district, in Bangor and in Sydenham Hill, a suburb of London. From the centres we had made almost daily excursions, taking picnic lunches. In the evenings we had sing-songs and every Friday a 'fancy dress evening'. Costumes needed imagination but little money. On these occasions we danced to the gramophone on the fine English lawns. We had a gay and carefree time and saw many things of beauty and interest. London made a great and unforgettable impression on me; I saw for the first time Westminster Abbey, St Paul's Cathedral, visited the National Gallery and rode on the open top of a bus to Hyde Park. Although we young people had much to talk about during these Holiday Fellowship vacations, political themes were never discussed. It would be very different today. While I was so tied to my bed at the beginning of the war these memories of my lovely holiday in England, and of the English people whom I had met at that time, occupied my thoughts, and the idea that all this would now be severed saddened me. From the beginning I had the feeling that Germany could not win the war and I had a pang in my heart whenever a victory was won and all the flags came out. It was considered unpatriotic not to put out a flag on these occasions. The only person in my family who had always concerned himself with politics was my brother-in-law Julius. He particularly criticized the pompous speeches made by the German Kaiser and the rest of the family agreed with him. Julius even knew the Kaiser personally, since as a teacher of classical languages and Director of the Humanistische Gymnasium in Homburg he was of course greatly interested in the excavation of the Roman Camp at the Saalburg, near Homburg, a project near to the Kaiser's heart. Therefore my brother-in-law was on one occasion invited with some other gentlemen to lunch at the Royal Castle in Homburg, the Kaiser's holiday residence. To the astonishment of the family, he recounted with irony how, when the Kaiser, who ate quickly, had finished, the servants removed the plates from all the other slower eaters. The critical attitude of the family certainly did not stimulate enthusiasm for the war in us at home.

Yet one saw the enthusiasm in the faces of youngsters, who after a short training came in their new uniforms through Frankfurt on the way to the front. They were greeted and regaled in the Frankfurt big railway station which was a large transit station for the western front. The poor young men, they had no idea of what lay before them!

In the beginning of the war, because of my pleurisy I was at home for three months. After that I was able to continue my studies in Frankfurt; for Frankfurt had meanwhile acquired a university. It was called the Johann Wolfgang Goethe University. Botany and zoology now began to interest me greatly. We had very good lecturers in these faculties, Professor Martin Möbius in botany and Professor Steche in zoology. The lectures of these two and their practical courses gave me an insight into these subjects which aroused my enthusiasm and encouraged me to read the works of Lamarck, Darwin and other great scientists and to study the scientific journals with interest. In this the Senckenberg library was a great help. I was especially pleased to attend the botany colloquium where we had to give papers on the latest contributions to the literature. This was the 'school' in which I first learned to speak freely and take part in discussions, for the mere reading of a paper did not please Professor Möbius. In 1915 I asked Professor Möbius for a theme for my doctoral thesis. The title was 'The dimensions and constitution of cell nuclei with particular reference to classification'. I now worked for two years in the botany laboratory, except for the hours during which I attended lectures. Professor Möbius was a fine distinguished personality of the greatest integrity and yet he was very amiable, open, outspoken and approachable. He had an extensive botanical knowledge and was also widely versed in many other disciplines. He made fine water colour paintings from nature and illustrated his own writings himself; he still read classical Greek. He was small, looked insignificant and was sometimes very silent. Only on closer acquaintance did one recognize his quite distinguished and noble character and then saw that he also had a subtle, dry humour. I appreciated him more and more, first as a teacher and later as a father-figure and friend. He had another special characteristic; he did not appear to age. At a relatively old age he still wrote scientific papers and published a history of botany of such fundamental value that it was republished only a short time ago.

In this period of my studies I went to and fro between the botanical gardens and the university. I collected the material I thought I needed from the gardens and the associated greenhouses. Then I fixed the parts of the plants which interested me, which in accordance with the usual practice were embedded in paraffin wax. Then microtome sections were cut, treated in the usual way and eventually they were stained and examined under the microscope. I made many drawings to establish the structure of the cell nuclei in the embryonic, growing and mature tissues. I also investigated plants which had been grown under varying conditions. All this and the study of the relevant botanical and zoological literature gave me great pleasure.

At this time only a limited number of students were to be found in the institutes and lecture halls. They were either girls or young men unfit for military service, for a war was raging and the male youth of the country was either in the field or in the trenches. Therefore there was a pleasant atmosphere between the few who came and went in the laboratory, which resulted from the close association. Views were exchanged and the results of investigations were shown to each other. The professor came and went and his friendly quiet manner promoted a harmonius atmosphere. His criticism spurred one on, his occasional appreciation gave pleasure. In these quiet peaceful surroundings one could sometimes forget the whole ghastly war. But the reports in the papers, the special editions, the letters from the front, the appearance of flags brought the whole terrible situation of our fatherland, indeed of Europe, vividly back to our minds. We wrote letters to the services, sent packages to the front, containing smoked sausage, small books and such things. In the next letter from the front Paul would write how fine the excellent sausage tasted with the 'Kommisbrot'. The list of the fallen became longer; one heard that an acquaintance, the brother or friend or secret fiancé of another friend would not return. One had assumed at first that the war would soon be over, but it lasted longer and longer. My younger brother Otto who took part in the battle of the Marne as a doctor was posted as 'missing'. Letters to him and his few personal possessions were brought to us by the postman with the note 'returned, missing'. For three long weeks the family suffered dread and anxiety. Then a short note came from him saying that, slightly wounded, he had been picked up as a prisoner by the English. Now at definite intervals, we had short letters from him from which we learned that he was alive and well. Also we were allowed to send him short notes from time to time. Finally before the end of the war, as a doctor, he was exchanged through Switzerland and sent home to the family.

In the first and second year of the war the food situation was still quite good. About 1916, because of the Allied blockade, shortage began to be felt and continued through 1917 reaching its worst towards the end of the war. We ate a kind of swede (*Kohlrüben*) ordinarily fed only to animals; and dried vegetables which contained sand, impossible to remove by washing, which grated in the teeth. The sparse bread ration became progressively poorer in quality. There was no longer any coffee or tea. We drank herbal brews and the men smoked 'herbal tobacco' (jokingly referred to as 'the German wood'). Everywhere wartime recipes were recommended. Once my good friend Minna, overjoyed with her discovery, brought us a little packet labelled 'Morning Drink'. Boiled with water, a brown fluid was produced, containing a suspension of undefinable particles. My mother bought secretly a white powder which was foisted upon her as flour. She baked a cake, with what other ingredients I don't know, but in any case an inedible stone-like lump came out of the oven. Even if it was partly flour which my mother bought in the paper bag, the swindler who sold it to her had mixed in a good portion of plaster of Paris. Such happenings had a certain comic touch. At this time my sister, who lived with Julius at Homburg, purchased a goat. She was housed in a nearby farm. Anny herself milked her daily and looked after her; it was proved that the milk of a clean goat did not taste 'goatish', but was quite drinkable and even goat butter could be made from it. My sister had also rented a small garden where, with great skill and much care, she grew cabbage, beans, peas, lettuces and even a few potatoes. All this was very necessary, for my brother-in-law was a tall well-built man, whose clothes hung loosely on him after a few years of war, he had become so thin. This garden bounty of my sister's sometimes reached us when she visited us and carried a heavy basket, filled with all kinds of fine vegetables, up our many stairs. I myself, who was very slight as a girl, never weighed more than 100 pounds at that time and had become too weak to take part in my favourite botanical excursions. Most people then had, or acquired, connections with people in the country. They went out into the country with rucksacks and begged at the farms for food (of course they paid well for it) and they returned with potatoes, flour and other victuals. This very wide-spread activity was called 'hamstern'. There were indeed few families who did not have secret and legally forbidden sources of supply. We did not 'hamster', but my brother Carl who was the head physician of a large hospital for infectious diseases in Inor, in France, gave several nursing sisters who travelled home on leave through Frankfurt food parcels to take along; these were faithfully handed over to my mother. Once we were in the princely state of having several joints of salted and smoked pork. Allegedly, there were state-employed officials who were

College Years

empowered to search for contraband foodstuffs in private houses; true, they never visited us. But as a precaution, this treasure was kept for some time in our piano, until it was all consumed.

In 1917 when I had passed my doctor's examination in Frankfurt, I again studied for one summer term in Göttingen; the students could eat there at a midday meal, organized by the university, for 50Pfg. As far as I remember, every day there was cabbage soup which satisfied for the moment, but was followed half an hour later by rumblings of the stomach! As I actually felt quite weak I went into the consulting room of a professor of internal medicine. He looked at me; I was thin and pale. He put a fatherly arm around me, then went to the desk and wrote a prescription: one pound of semolina, one pound of rice, half a pound of sugar weekly and half a litre of milk daily. He summed up the position and helped me greatly. My landlady had a secret supply of oil and also grew some potatoes. She gave me some of these and so I could sometimes make myself a splendid evening meal of boiled potatoes with salt and some oil.

As already mentioned I graduated on 15th January 1917 in botany, with zoology and mathematics as subsidiary subjects. I wore for the occasion a newly tailored costume and a brown silk blouse to match. The blouse had a flounce and was worn over the skirt, and naturally had long sleeves and a high neck. (I mention this because before the year of my graduation girls had come in black to their examinations like the men.) My mother had bought in advance a large flower pot of lilies of the valley, which was a little optimistic. But she was very happy when I returned from my oral doctor-examination with the mark 'very good'.

After an examination one always feels to some extent at a loose end, because one has been working steadily up to that date. Suddenly there is no more work to do. In addition, the term was half over and I could not attend new lectures. So I went to the professor of zoology and asked if I might work with him until spring, and he agreed. That winter was the coldest I have ever experienced, it was like Siberia; I think I remember that the temperature went down to $-30\,°C$. There was a coal shortage; the Senckenberg Museum and the associated rooms of the zoology institute could not be heated. But one small room, in which were terraria and aquaria, and the windows of which faced south, was kept agreeably warm. There I now worked daily with two other students. For us tables were set up with microscopes and simple instruments. We ran as quickly as possible from home through the streets to get out of the cold and then we warmed and sunned ourselves with the reptiles and fishes in our small work room. And again I came to a new world. I was studying single celled marine life which produced shells or a skeleton, such as the radiolaria. The professor brought me the material for this and I made numerous drawings of the wonderfully constructed shells and skeletons such as Haeckel depicted so well in *Kunstformen der Natur*. The professor also frequently brought me glasses from the Museum collection in which, for example, medusae hovered; and he taught me to make life-like drawings of these strange and interesting shapes.

I was not a good pupil in the drawing and painting lessons at school. In particular I was a failure when the teacher gave us a fairy story or a story of something imaginary to illustrate, as a task. But even as a child I liked drawing butterflies, beetles, leaves and flowers from nature and colouring them in water-colours. I also liked perspective drawing at school. Unfortunately, in those lessons the teacher did not allow us to follow our individual tastes. As in the piano lessons at the Frankfurt conservatoire, I was always discouraged. True, I was far from being musical, but I was certainly not like Carl to whom music was just a noise. I listened to it with pleasure (especially classical music). I also played with great enjoyment the little sonatinas of Mozart and Beethoven and short preludes of Bach which are suitable for children. But my teacher was very ambitious; she expected me to play without music. Also it hurt me deeply, that she did not believe me when I assured her that I practised for an hour every day. I had to write down from which time to which time I carried out my exercises daily. Distrustful teachers are especially discouraging. I gave up piano lessons when I was about fourteen; but I was very sorry later that I could not produce a little music from the piano for my own satisfaction and pleasure. With encouragement I would have practised much more as a child and acquired some technique.

The pleasant period of working in the zoological institute came to an end in spring 1917. As I mentioned before, I went again for a summer term to Göttingen and there attended mainly lectures in mathematics by Professors Hilbert, Runge and Caratheodory. In winter I returned again to Frankfurt for the 'Staatsexamen' or examination for teachers in higher schools, which I passed in autumn 1918. My subsequent pedagogic training I obtained at the Schillerschule and associated Mädchengymnasium in Frankfurt. The Staatsexamen, because of my experiences related earlier, rather exhausted me and I spent the following day in bed. Then I received a letter from Minnie, the sister of my friend Paul, informing me of his death. I was deeply shocked and saddened.

The then 23-year-old young man served first in the Engineer Corps and

College Years

in the final stage of the war had been an air observer. He had volunteered for a special mission three days before a last leave would have been due. He was shot in the thigh, and although the pilot landed on the German side of the lines five minutes later, he bled to death before he could be taken to hospital. In those days there were no blood transfusions or he could perhaps been saved. Four weeks later the whole war was over.

Paul was 18, I 21 years old when we met right at the beginning of our first term. The professor of mathematics had called the new students together for a preliminary talk. I remember that we stood in two groups in the main hall of the university building. On the one side stood a biggish group of young men, on the other side about eight young women, of course I among them. Paul had a good look round and then came over to our side after the professor had finished. He introduced himself and asked me if I would allow him to accompany me to my home. I had no reason to refuse this request to the decent looking, polite young man. We went together over the 'Göttinger Wall' to my domicile; we talked together about this and that in a lively but most innocent manner. From then onwards Paul accompanied me every day on my way home from the lectures. He seemed to know my time-table by heart and was always waiting for me at the exits of the lecture halls. He was not the only one with whom I became acquainted, but he was the only one whom I liked and to whom I gave my friendship. I felt his youthfulness strongly and regarded myself as older and more experienced, but he had something bright, open and endearing to which I reacted and in spite of his youthfulness he was of a serious disposition. He was uncommonly well balanced and of great integrity and honesty; his sister Minnie whose acquaintance I made soon was one year his senior and seemed to me of a similar kind of character. Paul seemed never to change in his faithfulness towards me, though he understood without words that I could not quite reciprocate his feelings and that all I could give him was friendship and a sisterly affection.

The great innocence that induced, in the year 1914, the best youths of Germany, England and the other nations involved to volunteer for war service in order to defend their countries and, if necesssary, to make the supreme sacrifice, is remarkably expressed in the war letters of young Paul. I kept them for so many years and I would like to quote some of them. They show that the young student underwent a mental change during this period and developed more insight and greater manliness.

Here then, follow excerpts from some of Paul Pignol's letters, which, written in a time so different from the present one, and yet just as tragic

Memoirs

with regard to human misunderstanding, seem to me of historical interest.

12.11.1914

You must not be resentful that you have not heard from me since my sudden departure from Göttingen. It was a very disturbed time until I had reached the stage of being introduced to the secrets of the Pioneer Corps. On the twelfth day of mobilization I was taken into the local Pioneer battalion but had to wait anxiously for a month for call-up until I was accepted. Now I have been here just two months but I have no prospect of going into active service before Christmas. I am pleased that I have arrived here, for the pioneer service is the best for someone with interests in engineering. If only we could get out and show the British our quality and let them feel its weight! It is indeed fine to live at such a time, serious and difficult though it is.

22.12.1914

We have recently fought an action like Yprés on a small scale, in that we dug in at the best positions and attempted to storm the enemy position from them. I wish you could only see such a position; from the outside almost nothing to be seen but inside the finest dug-outs with all possible comforts, almost bomb-proof. That is a great piece of pioneer work.

Revanjfala (Neudorf, 6.12.1915)

Many thanks for your welcome packet that reached me, or rather that I reached again only in Hungary. We have in fact left this front, marched back again through the whole of Serbia and here came up to our post which could not travel so fast and now wait in the middle of the Hungarian Pussta for despatch to another combat area.

You are quite right, I can no longer imagine an ordered life with scientific research. A fresh, successful war of movement, such as we have experienced in the last two months, with all its disorder, the living and caring only for the moment with complete absorption in the present task, without meditating and speculating, with its continually changing impressions is as good as can be imagined. That is the finer side of soldiering. For four weeks we have acted as ferrymen over the Danube. Sometimes it made one think of the poem

'Zelte, Posten Werdarufer
Lustige Nacht am Donauufer'

Often however we find the Danube waves too much for us! Our fragile ferries swing so strongly backwards and forwards that even the experienced pioneers became seasick. The fears of the horses and drivers faced with such waters cannot be described. We've had more battles with nature here than with the Serbians. In the Morava, which because of such high waters flowed more rapidly than I have ever seen it before, we tried several times to set up ferries and bridges and only succeeded at the fifth attempt. Unfortunately some of the men were drowned. With the tipping of my pontoon I just escaped. Then one experiences how truly helpless man is. After crossing the Danube, when we had come up to our division, there was considerable work for us as we went forward on the destroyed road bridges (these bridges are very frequent in this mountainous country). In addition to this there was bad weather, the unaccustomed climate, very warm by day, rain and frost by night. But no lack of food and other necessities for every day living since there was plenty to requisition from the not-so-poor Serbians, better off than we had imagined them. We have now come to the mountain pass of Prejwolar, south from Kursumlije, and unfortunately could not take part in the last battle. But we shall never forget this wonderful time of the war in the Balkans.

Wolhynien, 11.9.1916.
I have never enjoyed the Pioneer service so much as at present. I have considerable scope for work on mines. The Russians dig saps against us and it is all a matter of who is the quicker. This underground war has a peculiar fascination; it is exciting and sinister...

12.2.1917
We are still carrying out a boring trench warfare in Wolhynien and in the long autumn and winter have adequately prepared for any Russian offensive against Kowel. The Wolhynien marshland is monotonous and bleak, and the everyday sameness of trench warfare is wearisome and enervating and it is difficult to find something to compensate for this...

Karlshorst, Flight Division Lubiko, 30.12.1917
Forgive me for not having written to you for so long a time. I have been on the move nearly continuously and not come to rest. In November I was in Göttingen but, to my great sorrow, heard you were no longer there. You have now brought your studies to a definite con-

clusion. I, on the other hand, during this time have been rather hindered. Now of course my technical interest is alive again for I have taken up the air observers' course and now learn wireless telegraphy, photography and get to know of the latest technical inventions while the theoretical instruction in atmospheric science, aircraft and engines remind me of my time with Prandtl, who is now working in his aerodynamic laboratory for aviators.

Work on dug-outs became in time rather too boring, so early in 1917 I reported to the air corps, actually to become a pilot. From the Galician offensive I then came in Brest-Litovsk to an army aircraft centre and there for the first time enjoyed the splendour of flying. Indeed it is indescribable how wonderful it is and who has once known it can never forego it, and now I am here in an Aerial Photography Command near Berlin, to learn the special details of photography. Unfortunately the end of my instruction is not in sight and I fear that I might not be ready by the time peace is concluded. But I should like very much to give Tommy, in time, my 'blessing' from above...

On 25th October 1918 I received from Minnie Pignol the shocking news of Paul's death, of which I have already spoken. She was herself very ill at the time and sent me only a short note. However, later I received several letters from her with more detailed reports. From these letters I concluded that she shared Paul's patriotic feelings and opinions.

The image of this gifted fine young man, who died so tragically on the threshold of life, remained with me throughout my life as a symbol of the terrible, monstrous injustice which the states inflict on their citizens. "Thou shalt not kill", we learned as one of the ten commandments in childhood. But the states can perpetrate mass murder without even being brought to account. How can politicians, elder statesmen, prime ministers take on the responsibility to send millions of young men to their certain death? In the different periods of my life I have asked myself again and again how it is possible that humanity is confronted with this terrible, outrageous crime?

In the first place it is the education of the children through the ages and in all countries of the world which influences the young people in their belief that they have to sacrifice themselves for their fatherland. The old Romans impressed it on their youths in the well-known quotation: 'Dulce et decorum est pro patria mori'. But it is neither sweet nor is it a glorious honour. It is a much greater achievement to live and to work for the 'pursuit of happiness' and for the progress and happiness of one's fellow men. The children of different nations, races and cultures play with each other if they have the opportunity. They do not discriminate according to descent, race or nation or even colour. The school history books inspire everywhere the children with prejudices against other nations. When I came to England I learned that Wellington was the celebrated victor of the battle of Waterloo. In Germany I had learned that Blücher won the battle. My Swiss friend, Professor Mooser, pointed out to me that Blücher's contribution was essential for the outcome of the battle. Of course, grown-ups are not always correctly informed by those in power. And during a war the information is even less correct than in peace-time, for patriotism has to be upheld.

We may well ask whether this vicious circle cannot be broken somewhere. Will man always be his own worst enemy? Can we see any sign of hope? In any case there are great differences when one compares the youth of today with those who fought in the First World War. The latter are by no means the innocent lambs we were; the students are interested in politics and belong to political organizations; they discuss the happenings in their own country and throughout the world; they demonstrate, for example against war, against racism. Youth expresses openly its opinion which cannot be ignored, and has more self-confidence in encounters with adults. Youth no longer accepts unquestionably what the politicians say, the doctrines of patriotism and the pronouncements of the Church.

There are many other signs that show that the youth of today is different from that of 1914. Today, for example, a considerable number of young people volunteer to go to underdeveloped countries to work there and assist in their development. Also people travel much more, especially the young, who see how the rest of the world lives. Of course, there is a reverse side to this. There are more hooligans among young people than formerly and more exhibitionism in behaviour and dress. There are said to be more juvenile delinquents. But is this only the dark side of the much brighter appearance of our youth? We reproach young people for not recognizing the authority of the older generation. But why should they accept the authority of a generation which brought about so much unhappiness in the world? We hope that present-day youth will be better equipped to help to improve the world when they have to take over.

Still, other signs of the times can be looked upon as rays of hope. Even if we are not politically well-informed—and perhaps this would hardly be possible—we quickly learn of many tragic happenings. An earthquake, a flood, a tornado, a famine anywhere in the world is brought home to us;

we see pictures of all the horror on television, we hear of it on the radio and read about it in the papers, we learn of the crimes that are comitted, we see pictures of rebellions, of wars, of the suffering of the civilian population. True, we don't hear and see everything which happens in the world, but the horrors of the world are part of our everyday life! And that's a good thing.

Moreover our weapons, our technical resources for destruction, have become so frightful that it is improbable that governments will so lightly start a war such as followed the assassination at Sarajevo. However, we must remember and therefore be afraid that everything that has been produced in the way of murder weapons has at some time or other been used for murder. It may also be asked whether the ever increasing populations of some countries create a tension which, like the electrical forces in the atmosphere, triggers off storms, fostering the outbreaks of wars. Sometimes there must be and can be a restriction in the numbers of births, whether through the 'pill' or by some other means, for otherwise in the forseeable future life in this world and the enjoyment of life, to which we have a right, will be made impossible for us.

CHAPTER III

Senior Teacher in Dresden

AFTER THE STAATSEXAMEN I had to spend one year as a probationer at the Schillerschule in Frankfurt. My task consisted mainly in being present at the lessons of various other teachers. From time to time I had to give a lesson myself under the supervision of an older teacher and the director of this school. This was followed by a discussion and criticism. Because of the presence at my own lessons of another teacher and the director I was never confronted with the difficult problem of discipline which every beginner has to overcome. I was of the opinion that I had not learned during this year how children should be taught or rather how I myself was going to tackle the problem of teaching children. I found out later that one can learn this only by one's own experience. It is also necessary that one possesses love and understanding for children. No method, however sophisticated it may be, can make a good teacher out of a person unsuited for this task.

Round about Christmas 1918 I had a severe attack of scarlet fever. At that time I was alone at home with my dear old parents. After the first two weeks when I had a consistently high temperature, I recovered visibly. I was lovingly looked after by my mother who spoilt me considerably; I could order for my meals what I liked best and my every wish was fulfilled. As I had been forbidden by the doctor to read myself my mother read aloud to me. So she read to me in time the whole of *Grüne Heinrich* by Gottfried Keller, which I enjoyed greatly. My mother had such a beautiful, sonorous voice of a simple and yet very warm timbre that I asked her frequently to read poems to me. She read without any pathos and yet full of expression. I cannot remember that I ever heard anybody read more beautifully, more warmly and with such simplicity and yet with all the nuances that a poet could wish for.

As I had to remain at home for six weeks and was not allowed to have any visitors, I remember this quiet and yet stimulating time with great gratitude, but also with a certain melancholy and almost home-sickness, for afterwards when I went out into the world by myself I was always more or less alone and had to fight my own battles. My husband once said to me, "Nobody has ever wanted to look after you so well as I did, except your mother". The affection and care of a good mother is a viaticum that lasts all through life.

After I had passed my year as a probationer and the examination at the end of it in 1919, I applied for a post as a senior teacher at the Nolden private school for girls in Dresden. My journey to Dresden so soon after the First World War was rather an adventure. At that time parts of Germany, especially near Frankfurt, were still occupied by the Allies. In Hanau our express was held up and French soldiers with fixed bayonets came aboard and drove us all out. In particular I still see before me a poor woman travelling with two small children. In addition to them and a bag she was also loaded with two large loaves of bread. Soon the amiable station master came out of his office to us on the platform, spoke words of cheer to us and said he would stop the next train for us. This happened and we continued our journey. I believe I was almost 36 hours on the way for the train went slowly and in Leipzig I had to wait several hours for a connection to Dresden. This last journey was also slow and the train stopped frequently. My large trunk had been sent to Dresden by freight train. When I opened it at my new domicile I found that a pair of new shoes and stockings had been taken out of it by a thief, but fortunately all my books, note-books and old clothes had been left untouched. A room had been taken for me in Dresden which was so small that I had to sit close to my wash stand, my bed taking up all the rest of the room! A change of accommodation was necessary. I looked round. However, neither the second nor the third room I rented was satisfactory. Eventually, I found an attractive room at the 'Waldschlösschen' near the Elbe with a very pleasant Baurat's family. The Baurat (an architect) had built the house for himself and his family. The elderly couple gave me the room vacated by their married daughters. It was very pleasant and friendly with a small settee and easy-chairs and with polka-dotted muslin curtains. The bed stood in a sort of alcove closed off from the room by a curtain so that the room itself looked like a sitting-room. From the room a door led to a small separate compartment fitted with shelves. There I could keep my trunks, my cooking utensils and my crockery. I could get water from a tap in the corridor outside my room and I could even use a gas stove fixed to the wall in the corridor. I was very well satisfied with these lodgings, in particular because my landlady was very pleasant and obliging. I assumed that they had been obliged to let a room in their large house and were glad to have me as a lodger.

Dresden was a wonderfully beautiful city; the laying waste of cities had not yet come to pass in the First World War and attacks on the civil population had not yet been planned, and although Frankfurt had experienced a few bomb attacks (once a bomb fell into our front garden and all the windows of my parents' house were smashed) at that time the British airmen could not penetrate so far east. Thus Dresden had not suffered during the war. The Brühl Terrace was one of the most beautiful walks along the bank of the Elbe. From there could also be seen the architecturally very fine Hofkirche which, like the famous Zwinger, derived from the golden age of Dresden. Also I frequently visited the treasures of the art gallery, where in one special room the famous Sistine Madonna of Raphael hovered over the clouds. Dresden also had good opera but I could not go very often because I had to teach twenty-six hours a week for a modest salary. I taught physics, chemistry and biology in the upper school and arithmetic in the middle school. Although director Bojunga of the Schillerschule, where I had received my pedagogic training, assured me that with my composure I would have no trouble with discipline, he was greatly mistaken. In the first place I felt very uncertain with my little experience of teaching. Children immediately sense a teacher's uncertainty so of course I had troubles. However discipline is the first requisite for successful education and teaching. In addition I had to work very hard during my first year of teaching, for I had never taught these subjects before, so I had to prepare myself in theory and practice for every lesson. That is I had to practise for myself with every experiment I showed the children so that everything went well. I also had to become familiar with the apparatus, the motor, switchboard, and so on, without any help. This hard work wearied me so much that each Sunday afternoon I had to go to bed to collect enough strength for the coming week. The second and third years at the Nolden school I found much easier and I had no further problems of discipline. I had gained the necessary self-confidence.

In addition to the lessons I now did all sorts of things together with the children, which pleased them and me. Some of them accompanied me on botanical field work collecting wild flowers. Many of them came with me to open spaces when it was dark early in winter, to become better acquainted with the constellations with the help of a star-chart. A number of them worked one afternoon voluntarily in school, where in pairs, they carried out experiments in physics or chemistry or observed and drew sections of parts of plants under the microscope. I had prepared instructions which the children could easily follow and they exchanged tasks so that each pair worked through all of them. Thus we became very good friends. There was great excitement in the class when I asked the children to describe experiments in simple sentences; no teacher had ever asked them this before! But it was my opinion that there had to be practice in expressing oneself in German in all school subjects; for it is important that the adult should be able to use his or her mother tongue as an instrument capable of expressing thoughts and observations. I had the experience later that many students were quite helpless when it came to writing out a thesis and needed a great deal of assistance. And how pleasant it is when people can write interesting and descriptive letters.

It was clear to me that in the arithmetic class in the middle forms constant practice was necessary. So I devised a sort of game which kept the children continually on the move. If a child gave the right answer it moved to the right-hand side of the classroom. If the answer was wrong it had to stand on the left-hand side. There was also the chance of moving up or down the rows. I have forgotten the exact rules of the game, but the physical movement and the mental exercises prevented any lassitude and the whole lesson was looked upon as a game rather than as work by the children. Half the class was in tears when I left the school in 1922.

The Nolden school was a private school, that is, the school fees which were paid by the parents had to suffice for maintaining the school, new equipment and for the salaries of all the staff. These last were very modest and I believe that the caretaker, who with his wife had to keep the school clean, received a very small amount. He and all his family lived free of charge in a gloomy basement of the school. Both he and his wife worked very hard; the wife and the children were pallid and once when I went down into their flat to discuss something I saw the youngest child lying in a cot and little bugs ran across his head. (I must add here that at that time Dresden was known to be infested with bed bugs in many parts.) I was very sorry for these caretakers, for they were honest and hard working folk, who were underpaid by Miss Nolden just as were her staff. She could not have a social conscience. Otherwise she could not have been Head of such a private school.

Senior Teacher in Dresden

The whole enterprise was an unsocial undertaking. The parents who sent their children there belonged to a social level which thought itself better than the middle class who sent their children to the ordinary schools (*öffentliche Schulen*) and paid only a small fee. The communities or the state paid the balance. The ordinary schools had better facilities and better teaching staff, who were also better paid. Thus the private schools served only those circles who wished to be apart from the rest of the population on whom they looked with prejudice. Very likely the parents of my pupils were also anti-Semitic and the Head would not have engaged me as a Jewish teacher. A colleague and friend of mine told me that Miss Nolden showed her my photograph which I had sent in with my application on request and brought up the question of my origins. Yet it was decided that according to my papers I was of the Protestant faith and it should be left at that, since it satisfied the requirements of the parents.

By the way, it was in Dresden that I myself made my first and only acquaintance with bed-bugs and that at my nice lodgings. One day I found a bug in my bed and told the Baurat's wife. She was not surprised but apologized and said that the maid who lived on the same floor as I had brought them in. We arranged for me stay for a week with a friend and in the meantime the place should be 'debugged'. I came back, looked behind all the pictures and still found one little survivor. It transpired that only the maid's room had been fumigated but not mine. Yet the landlady believed there were now no more bugs and offered to test this by sleeping for a week in my room. When I came back once again, all was well. I just had to find the last surviving little bug!

In the year 1920 I had a severe attack of the 'Spanish influenza', to which a large part of the population fell victim in Germany and all over the world. I lay in bed in my room with a fever for a fortnight, my landlady and the maid looking after my needs. I was a member of the health insurance society (*Ortskrankenkasse*) so the insurance doctor living in the neighbourhood was called in. He sat at my bedside and talked to me for a little while without ever examining me. When the fever left me I got up; my landlady suggested that I ate my dinner with her and her husband, an invitation I gladly accepted. Mornings and evenings she brought me what I needed. I still felt weak, but thought I had to work again, so I went to the same doctor in his surgery hours. He merely said, "So you want me to certify that you are fit?" I said "Yes". Again he failed to examine me. On returning home I collapsed on the stairs, which was not surprising. Fortunately, when I was ill, the charming matron of the Diakonesses Hospital, a friend of my brother Carl, visited me from time to time. She said, "I will make an appointment for you to be examined by our professor". He examined me thoroughly and said, "Your lungs and heart are still slightly affected and without a proper convalescence you could feel the effects of this for the next few years." He got in touch with my health insurance society. There I was again examined and the doctor there made the diagnosis appear even more serious than did the professor; I think he was sorry for me. I received sick benefit for another four weeks. Miss Nolden said, "We won't have a substitute for you, you will make up the lessons for the children when you return and your salary will continue". The professor proposed that I should go to the convalescent home of the Deaconesses' Order in the Erzgebirge. I paid there 8 Marks a day, which I could now well afford. It was mid-winter, cold and sunny. The treatment consisted of strict rest; mornings and afternoons, wrapped in blankets and provided with hot water bottles I would lie in a deck chair, in the sunshine, on the verandah. I was not alone; a charming young nurse lay beside me and chatted to me. I thought the innocent young nurse needed some more education, so I read *Othello* with her. We were well cared for; we each had our own room; the company was pleasant and interesting. In the last week I was able to go for walks, had no longer to lie down during the day and felt quite recovered. I now quickly let my family know; I had not informed them of my sickness so far, because I knew how anxious my parents would have been and it had all come right in the end.

The Dresden post, the first I had applied for, I had accepted quickly because I did not want my parents, who had given me such a generous education, to have the responsibility of keeping me any longer. Yet slowly the conditions at the school became clear to me, that is its drawbacks; the prejudices of the parents, the not exactly idealistic outlook of the headmistress, who treasured me as a good energetic youngster whom she did not have to pay too much. The salary was especially inadequate when inflation came, because naturally the improvement in salaries of a private school lagged behind the rising prices to a greater extent than at the *öffentlichen* schools of the communities or the state. Also, so soon after the war there was still a definite shortage of food. I could not buy butter; it was too dear, but there was good dripping in the butcher's shops. This is the fat which remains after cooking sausages and often contained little fragments of sausage meat from burst sausages. I fed myself as cheaply as I could; but not badly. Some evenings I ate rice-pudding, cooked in the haybox which my sister had constructed for me, or I ate potatoes with a herring, also a good source of protein. At midday I used to visit an inn with two other women teachers, who were my friends. We called the inn the 'Coachmen's Pub' because it was frequented by coachmen and labourers. There was good 'family' cooking at this inn; doubtless the pleasant landlady herself was the cook; she also served at table. It was simple and wholesome but clean and cheap and the sort of people who went there did not disturb us at all. Once a man, slightly drunk, came into the inn, looked at me and said, "I would like to marry the little one at the table there on the spot!", an incident which amused us greatly. I can remember to this day the good roast meat with potato balls and the apple pudding which the landlady set before us. Afterwards there was a good cup of coffee.

All this would have been quite agreeable. But as I said, I was not very happy at school. Also teaching to a prescribed programme with the use of prescribed books and to a mixture of children of high, average and very slight abilities gave me no pleasure. The thought would come that year-in, year-out one would have to teach a similar selection of children with the same material.

I longed to be back in the laboratory, for the two years in which I had worked in the Botanical Institute to obtain my doctorate were my happiest years as a student. I resigned in 1921 after two years at the Nolden school, but withdrew my resignation again and postponed it until autumn 1922. My relations and particularly my brother-in-law Julius, whose voice carried weight in the family and who himself was a teacher, could not grasp that I wished to give up the teaching profession, which apparently offered such a safe existence. Julius expressed his opinion sharply; my sister who understood me better, did not wish to contradict; my parents remained neutral; but in Homburg I had to put up with misunderstanding and prejudice. But my mind was made up. Actually the matter was not half so tragic as it appeared, for the teaching profession would still have been open to me later. Even today, I believe I would have done better at an 'öffentliche Schule' than at the Dresden private school and that in time I would have become a quite good and satisfactory teacher, for I was not without teaching ability and dealing with growing children and adolescents gave me constant pleasure throughout my life. In my later scientific activities I have looked upon it as a great privilege that I always had to work with younger people. Even now in my old age it is the greatest source of joy to me that young people still come to me and I am very grateful for this. However, there is no doubt in my mind that research and university teaching appealed much more to me than school teaching.

In my summer holidays in 1922 I was in Frankfurt and there visited various scientific institutes and their directors to see if I could find a position anywhere. Among others I visited the Städtische Hygienische Universitätsinstitut. The director was on leave and was represented by the deputy professor, Braun, who was also the head of a department; when I explained to him that I wanted to leave the teaching profession and go into a laboratory again he merely said, "That is the crazy quest of our time". This struck me forcibly and unforgettably because it was so wrong in my case. But then he advised me to get in touch with the director, Professor Max Neisser, who was spending his short leave in his holiday house in Falkenstein in the nearby Taunus mountains. I wrote to him and he invited me to visit him, which I did. He spoke with me about half an hour and explained to me that in the autumn a post for a non-medical scientific worker would become vacant. On the return journey I wished to take the road which led from Falkenstein via the 'Hohe Mark' to Bad Homburg, to visit my sister in Homburg. Professor Neisser accompanied me along the beautiful woodland path leading up to the 'Hohe Mark'. He talked vivaciously, said that he did not want to see my testimonials—which no doubt were good—for he took little notice of testimonials. He also indicated that there might be a possibility of becoming a university lecturer within the medical faculty. I silently promised myself: I will do that.

After the summer holidays I returned to my post in Dresden. Up to the beginning of the autumn vacation, the date for which I had resigned my school post, I heard nothing more from the Hygiene Institute in Frankfurt. For the autumn holidays I was invited to Obernick, near Breslau by good friends of my brother Otto. They had there in the country a sanatorium for psychiatric patients. It was a very nice building with a special big flat for the leading doctor, to which was attached a large private garden. I was spoiled by the kindly doctor and his wife. There were all kinds of diversions such as picking fruit in the garden, walking, playing a pianola, a recently invented sort of mechanical piano, and the highlight—on clear nights we studied the moon through a telescope. Finally, after a most agreeable fortnight I took my leave and travelled back to my lodgings in Dresden. I needed a whole day to go from Breslau to Dresden, since because I had little money I travelled fourth class. Express trains had then no fourth class, only those passenger trains

Senior Teacher in Dresden

which stopped at all small stations had. Often on such meandering journeys I got into conversation with fellow passengers and on this journey I became friendly with a shoemaker, who invited me to a cup of coffee at an intermediate station. He would gladly have met me frequently in Dresden. He believed me to have a post as a maid servant there and I did nothing to disillusion him on this point! The Germans are—or were then—very inquisitive in such matters and wanted to know where one came from, was going, and who one was. As they had usually a preconceived opinion as to status I left them to their beliefs and travelled sometimes as an art student or as a maid and once as a midwife, to or from Dresden. The attempt to label me as a midwife was occasioned by nothing more than a white laboratory coat which lay in my suitcase on top of other things.

When I returned to my room in Dresden, I saw that they had forgotten to forward my post to Obernick, because a grandchild had arrived and this happy but distracting event had turned the household upside down. Among my letters one from Professor Neisser had already been lying there for a week. In it he said I should apply immediately for the post of a 'bacteriologist' at the Institute of Hygiene. I was shocked, because naturally the post which I desired so much could meanwhile been taken. I packed my trunk with all speed and what would not go in I put in a rucksack, on the outside of which was tied a hat and a frying pan. I caught the night express to Frankfurt and at seven o'clock in the morning I was on my parents' doorstep at 51 Reuterweg. My mother was rather shocked at the appearance of her daughter, but gladly gave me a good breakfast and after a refreshing hot bath and dressed in a manner more suited to a lady I arrived at the Institute of Hygiene in the Paul-Ehrlich-Strasse 40 at 9 o'clock. The worthy secretary Fräulein Kerschke told me that the 'Herr Geheimrat' was at a meeting and was not expected at the Institute before noon. I was on tenterhooks for another three hours. The interview with the professor was very short; he merely said, "Apply for the post at once". I had all my papers in order and sent in my application that same day. I received a favourable reply and entered on my new duties a few days later. It was a bit ironical that among the papers on which at that time the application and curriculum vitae had to be handwritten a large handmade star had been slipped which Professor Neisser returned with my papers, without comment. During my time in Dresden I was often alone in the evenings and then read aloud poetry such as that of Rilke or Stefan George or I occupied myself with tatting, also called 'Frivolitäten'. The finished masterpieces I kept between my foolscap papers.

CHAPTER IV

Städtische Hygienische Universitäts Institut in Frankfurt

ACCORDING TO MY NEW POST I was now a 'bacteriologist'. However, before I could take over my new duties I had first to learn bacteriology. Professor Neisser said, "You can learn all the theory of bacteriology and its methods in two years, but to become a bacteriologist requires 10 years!"

A small laboratory and an office were put at my disposal. The latter was pleasant with a writing desk and chair, bookcase and wash-basin with hot and cold running water. Between these two rooms, that is my laboratory and the office, was the rather large collection of bacterial cultures. I had a good microscope for my own use, all the necessary reagents and staining solutions as well as all the necessary glass equipment to hand. Incubators and apparatus were in the adjacent large laboratory where the ready-prepared nutrient media were also kept. There, in the large laboratory were the benches for a medically trained assistant doctor and several female technicians. The whole working atmosphere, and the possibility of being able to learn so many new things, pleased me very much. I could listen to all the lectures given in the Institute. I could make use of the library of the Institute and that of the director; and in the director's anteroom I could study all the new periodicals which the Institute took. I made myself at home in all the different departments of the Institute, for example, where tuberculous material, urine samples, blood from enteric infections, stools, etc. were examined for the various kind of bacteria pathogenic to man, until I learned all the pertinent methods. I became proficient in all the routine

Bacteriologist in Frankfurt

examinations which were then used at the Institute. Soon I was assisting in the preparations for the courses which were held at the Institute for medical students and also for scientists, and I also helped in the practical instruction of the students during the courses. Another one of my duties was that of procuring all the glassware, chemicals and so on which were used, and the issuing of these to the different departments. I had one of the technical employees of the Institute to help me in this. Then I had to supervise the preparation of autovaccines and the examination of water samples from the various sources which supplied Frankfurt with drinking water, and finally the examination of milk and yoghurt sent in by the dairies under municipal control. Later I supervised the preparation for courses and the maintenance of the culture collection. A technician helped me with these various duties. During the leave period of the doctor I had to take over his work. It was his duty to carry out serological (Widal reaction) and cultural examinations of blood from patients with typhoid, paratyphoid and other enteric infections as well as the examination of material sent for tbc diagnosis of tuberculosis. A woman and a man technician were available for this. All the usual methods, including serological reactions and tests on animals, were used. Thus I received a very thorough training in the methods used at that time in an institution set up for the examination of samples sent in by the doctors for bacteriological diagnosis. In writing this down in the year 1973 I ask myself if the present day bacteriologist can realize how widespread many infectious diseases still were in the nineteen-twenties in culturally developed countries, and how very necessary these tests were at the time. The changes that have taken place since, for example, in the distribution of diphtheria and typhoid fever (to name only two diseases), are amazing.

In the free time left to the assistant doctor and myself we could occupy ourselves with research. There was no lack of problems for our attention. If the daytime was not long enough we continued into the evenings. Day by day I looked forward to the laboratory work. My first investigation was concerned with the methods of testing disinfecting agents. Then one day in 1923 or 1924 we saw our first bacteriophages. The director or as we called him 'the chief', received from abroad a small ampoule containing bacteriophage together with a tube of the sensitive bacterium. We streaked the bacteriophage at different dilutions, together with the sensitive bacterium, on culture plates. The next day we saw for the first time the holes the bacteriophage had made in the culture lawn. This new discovery seemed almost like a miracle to us. The whole institute was called together to see it. As is well known, the bacteriophages were discovered in England and France during the war; therefore we in Germany did not become acquainted with them until a few years after the war had passed and we called them according to their discoverers the 'Twort d'Herelle phenomenon'. During the following years I worked myself for quite a time with bacteriophages; they are viruses of bacteria which can now be demonstrated under the electron microscope in a great multiplicity of forms. But then in the 'twenties we had no possibility of making them visible; we only recognized them by their effects. Afterwards I occupied myself with the variability of bacteria and with problems of their morphology, especially the effect of different substances on the shapes of bacteria.

The chief came into the laboratory almost every day. He was shown the results obtained from special samples sent in by the doctors and informed about the progress of our research. He often made suggestions for further investigations, which were sometimes pursued, or discarded if they were considered inappropriate. He had such an active intellect, with so many ideas, that by the next time he had forgotten at least half of them. But discussions and conversations with him were very stimulating and sometimes also amusing when he told us this or that incident from his eventful life. He loved to speak to us about his revered teacher, the famous Paul Ehrlich. The chief and his charming and intelligent wife invited us (that is the scientific staff of the Institute) at least once a year to Sunday luncheon. On these occasions, and also at social gatherings, for example after conferences, the chief revealed to the full his talent as a teller of anecdotes, for he was a great raconteur. His lectures were also frequently quite excellent; yet strangely enough he was not so good when he had to speak at scientific conferences. To my astonishment he once confided to me that he always had stage-fright; though on informal occasions he was very quick-witted and nearly always very amusing.

When, at nearly 30 years of age, I came to the Institute of Hygiene in Frankfurt, I was indeed not in every way experienced enough in life. So this period in Frankfurt did much to remedy that lack. I had to deal with so many different kinds of people; for instance, the male technician who was placed under my authority, although not then 60 years old, was prematurely senile, as I came to realize. He could not be employed to assist in bacteriological work. Once when I spoke to the chief about this, he said, "Anyone can work with a good assistant; it is an art to work with a bad one". I had learned a lesson; it gradually became comprehensible to me that the highly respectable man was an extremely good and reliable

Bacteriologist in Frankfurt

worker in the time of Paul Ehrlich, that he was promoted to 'Präparator' and had the complete confidence of Ehrlich and his scholars. Professor Neisser had taken him over when he became director of the Hygiene Institute and was unwilling to discharge him until he had reached a pensionable age. He could always be employed for fetching and carrying and for preparing solutions etc. He was indispensable in dealing with our stocks of glassware and chemicals and in this respect most reliable. When this 'Biedermann' died in 1933 at the beginning of the Hitler regime I went to the funeral and saw how the tears ran down the cheeks of my good chief and his wife, I expect in memory of old times.

My first technical assistant was intelligent but a cheeky hussy. She was obviously too much for the chief and at length had to be discharged. After she left us the chief came to me and asked, "Did she say good-bye to you?" "No", I replied. "Then I'm in good company", he remarked. My next technical assistant was a much more difficult problem for very different reasons. She was at the beginning of her forties, looked quite attractive and had a pleasant manner; she also seemed willing and industrious. But now and then it appeared as if she had a brain-storm. It might be that a water sample had been delivered; she had taken it, put it into the refrigerator and then for two days had completely forgotten about it. This and similar happenings became more frequent in the course of time. Nevertheless she was an experienced worker and well trained. I worried greatly about her. I spoke to the assistant and the chief; I was told I must be stricter with her and supervise her better. Yet she always seemed to slip through the net of my watchfulness. At that time we made a lot of autovaccines, i.e. for furunculosis and cystitis; the causative bacteria were cultivated from the material sent in by the doctor, pure cultures produced, filled into ampoules at suitable dilutions, killed off in a hot water bath and supplied to the doctor. These suspensions of bacteria were injected into the patients to stimulate them to produce antibodies and thus produce immunity against the cause of the disease. It was obvious to me that the preparation of a vaccine for injection into a patient could not be entrusted to an unreliable assistant. After many more or less sleepless nights I went to the chief and told him I could no longer put my signature to the cards which went with the ampoules to the doctors because if, for example, living bacteria such as streptococci should be injected into a person this could be fatal and I could go to prison. The chief merely said, "I cannot compel you to do this". A little later he returned to me and said, "I asked her unexpectedly if she were a drug addict, without hesitation she replied: 'No, I think you are mistaken"'. I found this rather naive, but I no longer signed her slips. Shortly afterwards something terrible happened. The other technical assistant who was responsible for examining urines for tubercle bacilli had injected as customary the sediment from a urine sample into two guinea-pigs. After a few days both animals died, which was most unusual and they were given to the assistant doctor for examination. He found the guinea-pigs had died from anthrax. How was this possible? Now followed a cross-examination. It appeared that I had given to my technician an anthrax culture to inject into mice, for in their course medical students were always given smears on slides from the spleen of mice which had died from anthrax so that they could stain and examine them microscopically. For this purpose my technician had borrowed a syringe from the technician dealing with tuberculosis; she had returned it *without boiling it* and placed it unsterile into the alcohol-glycerine mixture in which the technician entrusted with the examinations for tuberculosis kept her sterile syringes. The latter had assumed this syringe to be 'sterile' and had used it without qualms or an inkling of suspicion. As anthrax bacilli form spores which are difficult to kill, objects infected with them have to be boiled for at least a quarter of an hour. When these facts came to light the chief had to sit down, completely shocked, for such a thing should never happen in a well-run laboratory. I had a little feeling of triumph but was careful not to say anything.

A few weeks later the lady in question went on leave and after a further week the chief received a letter from the doctor of an establishment for the treatment of drug addiction. He was informed that this woman was staying there for a cure of her morphinism. It transpired that this technician was friendly with the matron in the private clinic of the professor of internal medicine. Both women were morphinists. The matron, of course, was in charge of the keys and the drugs came from the medicine cabinet of the clinic. Both unfortunate women were discharged; I know nothing of their later lives.

I had yet a second time to deal with drug addiction in the Institute of Hygiene. It is of interest to note that the person involved was a doctor, again somebody who had easy access to morphine. He was a young married man who came to us as an assistant doctor after having just undergone a 'cure'. We knew of this, but the director wished to give him a fresh chance out of the goodness of his heart. But it was of no use. He had a relapse and caused indescribable confusion. He mixed up the cards sent in by the doctors and the various cases. I tried to help to the best of my ability, but usually there was nothing for it but to ask the doctors for new samples. The young assistant doctor played only a 'guest role'; he also had to be dismissed.

In other ways also I amassed various kinds of noteworthy professional and human experiences in my post as bacteriologist at the Frankfurt Institute of Hygiene. The task fell to me to expel Pharaoh-ants, a small tropical ant introduced into Europe by shipping, from the Institute and later also from the Municipal and university hospitals, which formed a large complex of buildings in our neighbourhood. A very able man, a technician of the Institute, was allotted to assist me and the 'Gold-und Silber-Scheideanstalt' helped with the preparation of a toxic substance that could be added to a bait. The little reddish-brown ants built their nests inside buildings which were warm throughout from central heating and in places which were quite inaccessible. Our tests showed that a too strongly toxic bait was at first taken by the ants; but these ants soon died, and the bait was no longer touched by the others. The concentration of poison had to be so adjusted in the bait that the ants lived for at least another 24 hours and fed their larvae with the poisoned food. After we knew this we put down poisoned bait alternating with tubes containing only thick sugar solution. In the latter tubes there were always a number of ants stuck fast which showed us that they were still present. So now in all the rooms of the Institute from cellar to attic at fixed intervals of time tubes were put down until, after a few months, we had completely conquered the plague. It was indeed a plague, for when I first came to the Institute all the refrigerators stood with their feet in tins filled with water. Otherwise the ants would have penetrated the bacteriological plates kept in them. Sandwiches which we brought for our lunch could not be left wrapped up on a table or in our bags; otherwise they would have been invaded by ants. So we had a little device for hanging foodstuffs from the ceiling. As soon as a mouse died in a glass jar a trail of ants formed and five minutes later the dead mouse was overrun by ants. After the ant plague had been conquered in the Hygiene Institute we went to the municipal hospitals to free them, and in particular the big centralized kitchen, from the little beasts. When in the evening after work one went into the kitchen and switched on the light, the wooden blocks, on which the meat was cut and prepared, shimmered with ants. The ants were gradually expelled from these hospitals. The work required very conscientious distribution of the tubes over a long period of time, and even the smallest room could not be overlooked. The Institute employee, Mr Wilhelm Hoos, who helped me, was a most reliable man. He had previously worked with the chief during the

First World War, and became later the head of the Disinfection and Pest Extermination Unit of the municipal hospitals under the supervision of our chief. During the Hitler period he was dismissed because of his socialist leanings and especially because of his liberal attitudes. He was kept going with private work. After this time he was reinstated and was respected and honoured for his good work, of which he could be justifiably proud. His only son was his successor.

Among the unusual experiences which I had as a bacteriologist at the Hygiene Institute I must include my comings and goings to the Frankfurt abattoir. It became the fashion to work with bacteriophages and I also occupied myself with them. Some scientists took the view that the pancreas was responsible for their occurrence. We had a different opinion and in order to prove that sterile organs are free from bacteriophages, but those contaminated with the contents of the intestine contain them, I used for a time to visit the Frankfurt abattoir every Monday morning, accompanied by a technician of the Institute. Under sterile conditions I took the pancreas from freshly killed pigs and calves. The butchers soon knew me and treated us and our activities with consideration. After the killing and further preparation of the animals we could—for a small sum paid to the butchers—open up some of the animals under sterile conditions and take out the pancreas. I had learned to take off the skin in such a way that there was no incision on the underside, because for each cut which spoiled the leather we had to pay extra. When I had completely opened the animal I could extract the pancreas with my gloved hands. It was fun to be known at the abattoir and be greeted by the butchers. There were lively goings-on early on Mondays, and one had to be careful not to be brushed or hit by a pig passing on the conveyor. We achieved our scientific goal. Bacteriophages could not be obtained from sterile pancreas.

Another unusual experience was my acquaintance with prostitutes, who at that time were supervised as far as possible both medically and by the police, and who were admitted to a special department of the municipal hospitals when treatment was considered necessary. At this time we were interested in the cultivation of gonococci and especially in the preparation of nutrient media which seemed suitable for this purpose and particularly also for the improvement of the customary procedures. For this reason I visited this department frequently, in order to obtain the material directly from the patients. In this I was helped by the extremely capable woman doctor who looked after these women. I was greatly impressed by her and by the way she knew how to deal with these patients and the way she had won their confidence. She was not only concerned about their genital diseases but also their other needs. She cleared them from round-worms and cured them of tape-worms. It struck me forcibly that these poor women, although very uneducated, were not at all wicked and that they should be treated with kind firmness as this woman doctor did.

In this connection I am reminded of a strange experience that my youngest niece had during the terrible confused times after the Second World War, in Munich. She had no money and no roof over her head. She was there all alone 17 or 18 years old and had lost her job. She sat crying one evening in an inn. Then a prostitute came up to her and said, "Youngster why are you crying?" When the prostitute heard the reason she said, "Come with me, I can put you up and look after you until you have a job again and you won't be bothered". And so it was.

I believe that I enriched my knowledge of human nature greatly at that period in the Frankfurt Institute and thus acquired a certain ability in dealing with people. I was, so to speak, thrown into the community of the Institute without the vaguest idea of the personalities accidentally brought together in that place. I think I had to thank an unconscious instinct and perhaps also my inborn cautiousness that I sailed smoothly through all the rapids without a 'faux pas'. I did not know the relationship that existed between the director and the second professor who was in charge of the whole ground-floor department. The latter had started his career as assistant to the director, qualified as a lecturer under Neisser, became 'Ausserordentlicher Professor' and head of the ground-floor department under the sponsorship of the director. He was a good worker and a good scientist. He suffered from an inferiority complex for which he overcompensated. Unfortunately, he always felt himself to be at a disadvantage and antagonized the director in a way which sometimes became almost ridiculous. In contrast to him Professor Neisser was direct, outspoken and voiced his opinions without reservations. As a matter of course I supposed in the beginning that I had access to all the laboratories of the Institute including those of the ground floor and had already considered asking Professor Braun if I could attend in his department and learn the methods in use there. I was particularly concerned to learn the methods for the diagnosis of diphtheria, a disease still widely spread at the time. However, something kept me back from doing this and instead I asked Professor Neisser how I could learn these important methods. He suggested that cases already dealt with and preparations from them be sent up to me and he made the necessary arrangements. Of course I soon saw the fly in the ointment, for the hostility of the head of the lower department against the director soon also turned against me, and grew in the course of the years with the increasingly good opinion which the chief formed of my work and me. When I, a non-medical graduate, wished to qualify as a lecturer of bacteriology in the medical faculty the chief asked Professor Braun if he would act as co-referee for my thesis (*Habilitationsschrift*). The professor agreed, but when the matter was discussed at the faculty meeting he declined, saying that he was not sufficiently acquainted with the subject matter. This greatly annoyed the chief. The co-referee task was then accepted by Professor Gotschlich, the Heidelberger professor for hygiene and bacteriology, and the outcome was very satisfactory. Sometimes this domestic strife led to peculiar, almost comic situations. Once, when in the professor's opinion I had been unable to provide sufficient Petri dishes for his course, because in the years just after the war we experienced a shortage of equipment, he shouted at me over the house-telephone and to the horror of the male and female assistants in the big laboratory I also raised my voice. The result was extraordinary, the conversation continued in a normal, polite tone of voice. This was a new lesson for me. Actually by nature and upbringing I tended to be modest and shy. But in professional life one must, as far as possible, discard these qualities. My chief once said to me, "Who puts himself in the corner will stay in the corner". Later I often tried to impress on my own pupils this wisdom.

Wherever men and women, and particularly men and younger women work together and are in daily contact with each other, attraction between the sexes cannot be avoided. One sees or hears this or that, and perhaps has also one's own experiences. Under such conditions a young woman may find a young man whom she likes and marries. Young couples frequently meet in this way in Institutes and firms; that is all very well! But if a woman remains a spinster she can, I think, generally only have one of two things; either an affair or a career. The two do not go well together, especially if, as is often the case, the man is married with children and, on top of this, her superior. I always knew that I wanted a career. I naturally sensed that not everything was right around me. Only much later, when I had left, I heard which of the women (laboratory assistants) had had illegitimate children, who had once an affair with whom, etc. The old men when they have retired and if one is on good terms with them, love to gossip and tell tales out of school!

Here I could now give my views about the sex problem and compare the present day youth and the present so-called 'permissive society' with that of my youth. But on the whole one can truly say 'plus ça change, plus c'est la même chose'. Certainly, it is very wrong to bring unwanted children into the world; and as in all other human relationships everything is wrong which hurts and damages others. However, I believe that sexual behaviour and sexual relationships are entirely private matters. Different people behave in these things and also in other relationships quite differently, each according to his or her character. A good and intelligent friend, a venereologist, once said to me, "Never let your relationship with your friends be influenced by their sexual behaviour". Very good advice!

Now I return to my personal life during my time at the Frankfurt Institute. About six months after I had moved back from Dresden to Frankfurt my father died in his ninety-first year. He suffered sadly during his last year of life, but had then a peaceful death. From then until my emigration in 1933 I lived with my mother. As the flat in my parent's house was too large for us and I also wanted to live nearer to my place of work we moved to a housing estate near the Frankfurter Stadtwald on the edge of the city, in a friendly road 'Unter den Kastanien'. And indeed there were chestnut trees there! We had a fine three-roomed flat with a balcony and a maid's room on the ground floor. We always had a pleasant maid from the country. First there was Käthe, clean, friendly and industrious. And when the pretty young girl got married she said to my mother, "I'll send you my sister, Maria, you won't notice the difference!" This was so, except that Maria was plumper, and not quite so intelligent and pretty as Käthe. The maids went shopping with my mother and accompanied her on short walks in the woods; Mother was kind and motherly to them. My mother and I got along very well; this was due mainly to my mother; for she always considered my wishes. When I came home dinner was waiting to be served. In the evenings I often worked reading journals or preparing my lectures. Then she sat quietly in the same room with her needlework or her book and said not a word. I could bring home guests, they were always welcomed by her and they were always entertained with food and drink. Sometimes on Sundays we made an excursion in our pleasant surroundings. I made the plans but, of course, I saw to it that it was not too strenuous for her, because at the time of my father's death she was nearly seventy-five. We also had some of the most pleasant travels together and I could not have wished for a better travelling companion. I was the organizer who made all the arrangements. Thus we spent six weeks together in northern Italy in 1926. My then 78-year-old mother had never made such a journey, yet she enjoyed it as much as I did. The first night we spent in Lucerne in a pleasant hotel at the lakeside. That same evening we went across the beautiful and famous old wooden bridge. On the next day, May 9th, we arrived in Milan. It was a very late spring and there the women were still wearing fur jackets and boas. The journey through the Po Valley in the rather slow smoky train pleased me, for I felt we were now really in Italy. In Genoa we stayed three days. We admired the view of the beautiful town climbing up from the bay. Once I wanted to climb a hill much praised in *Baedecker* and I asked a young Italian the way. I had learned Italian for two years from a nice German-Italian woman. I was surprised when the young man accompanied me and appeared to lead me to a lonely place. Then he put his arm around me; it struck me that in Italy to address a young man is taken as an invitation. With some difficulty I broke away and ran down the hill.

From Genoa we travelled to Florence. How enthusiastic I was about the journey through beautiful, fertile Tuscany. The fields were so green and the vines planted around them interwove into each other as if they performed a round dance. Little villages, looking genuinely Italian, greeted us from the heights. In Florence we stayed in a Scandinavian Pension on the Arno. I had read up a few books and I had the city plan of Florence and most of the main streets firmly fixed in my mind. Generally in the mornings we went into museums and churches enjoying the works of art. The afternoons we often devoted to short excursions, such as a walk in the Boboli Gardens or to Fiesole and a Cistercian monastery. We visited the famous museums twice, also the Medici Chapel where each time we spent an hour as I could not tear myself away from the beautiful sculptures of Michelangelo. From Florence we went to the Riviera and spent two enjoyable weeks in Santa Margharita, making many excursions from there, such as to Portofino or in a small motorboat to Sestri Levante. We often took one of the fiacres kept for visitors, drawn by one horse, and went for a little drive. Usually in the evenings I ordered a half bottle of Italian white wine for our dinner. As my mother, although the wife of a wine merchant, did not like alcoholic drinks and at the most took them greatly diluted with water, I had the lion's share, and getting up from the table I enjoyed feeling the slight effect of the wine in my legs! The last fortnight of our Italian tour we spent in a small place called Gargnano on lake Garda. It was already mid-June and quite hot in the mid-day sun; but it was pleasant to sit in the shade near the lake, which in its great expanse and its waves reminded me of the sea. Near our hotel was a princely residence, with a house like a palace, surrounded by a wonderful park. Only the 'major domo' dwelt in it, and for a tip he allowed us inside the park. Many mornings we sat on marble benches under the large shady trees at the lakeside reading our books and behind us strutted peacocks, which for ornamental reasons were kept in the park. Otherwise we were quite alone there and felt like princesses. We made many trips by steamer and visited the various places around the lake. I must add that on this journey we also visited Pisa, Bologna and Verona. When in Verona I asked a passer-by the way in my best Italian. He replied in German, from which I concluded that I did not speak like a 'native' by a long chalk.

I also made other journeys with my mother. One summer we went to the Ticino, where we spent a few weeks in a little place called Montagnola, situated above the lake of Lugano, in a pleasant pension called Bellevue. There we became friendly with a similar couple, mother and daughter, who were from St Gallen. I went swimming and rowing with the daughter, while the mothers sat on the lovely terrace of Bellevue with their needlework. But often we took our mothers with us on steamer trips or short excursions to the charming places on the lakeside. My mother and I spent the last week of this holiday in Lugano-Paradiso and from there we went up Monte Salvadore and Monte Generoso, and to this day I remember the beautiful wild cyclamen we found growing on Monte Salvadore.

Often we visited my brothers, who were now married and had children. During my time in Frankfurt at the Institute of Hygiene my brother Carl lived in Zittau in Saxony where he was the director and chief physician of the municipal hospital. As he was extremely capable and a very considerate doctor he had also a very good private practice and people came from the whole district for consultation. My brother and sister-in-law had a beautiful house in Zittau and enjoyed having visitors, so we sometimes spent our holidays there. The surroundings, the Lausitz, are hilly and suitable for all kinds of walks and climbs.

My brother Otto was then in Königsberg as 'Oberarzt' (Registrar) of the university psychiatric clinic. Later he practised as psychiatrist in Königsberg. Königsberg, now under the Russians called Kaliningrad, then belonged to Prussia; it was a beautiful town and charming beauty spots like Kranz on the Baltic Sea could be easily reached from there. The journey from Frankfurt to Königsberg took 24 hours and went through Berlin. My mother and I usually travelled over night, by sleeper, to Berlin, taking from there a train to Königsberg in the early morning and arriving in the evening. I especially liked the Kurische Nehrung, the extensive tongue of land which encloses the Kurische Haff in the north and leaves open only a small passage to the sea at the eastern end. The much frequented beauty spot Nidden lies on the Nehrung where I spent many a holiday. Swimming in the Baltic in the summer was a great pleasure; I was a good swimmer and often swam far out to sea. First one had to be sure whether the current flowed towards the open sea or to the land. In the first case it was dangerous to swim too far out, in the second case one might well venture. In the evenings in fine weather we would hurry to the highest dune at Nidden to see the sun sink like a ball of fire into the sea. Not far from Nidden was Rositten, the famous bird sanctuary. A walk there was always rewarding; numerous sea birds were to be seen, nesting there in large numbers.

Once I met my brother Carl and we walked for several days along the Frische Nehrung, which is rather wider and more wooded than the Kurische Nehrung. From Königsberg Otto and I visited the fine Masuric Lakes. Since they were joined by canals one could go by steamer from one lake to the other. Less attractive was a long sea journey from Pillau on the 'amber' coast (Pillau is the port of Königsberg) to Swinemünde, from where we visited the island of Rügen. On this trip, which was to have been the highlight of the holiday, there was a terrible storm. We all three, that is Otto, his future wife and I were seasick, as we never were before or since, although I took many sea trips in later years. I greatly enjoyed wandering along the coast of the Samland with its steep escarpment, which was then East Prussian. This coast had the special attraction that the mixed woodland of deciduous trees extended right to the coastline which then sloped down steeply. A special sight in this area was a herd of elk which could be reached by hiring a small light, horse-drawn carriage; the driver knew where to find the herd by driving across the countryside and woods until we approached quite close to these proud splendid elks. They allowed the horses to come near to them but fled from men and cars.

Sometimes I travelled alone, without my mother. Most impressive were the holidays which I spent high up in Zermatt, in Switzerland, as I was able to make many fine excursions from there. At that time I also had the unique experience of climbing with a guide one of the four-thousanders of the alps. We climbed the Breithorn, 4170 m high. In the afternoon we ascended to the hut where we spent the night. At 2 a.m. the guide knocked at the door and at 3 a.m. we began the marvellous climb. Moon and stars were still in the sky; it was a quite clear night. Now dawn came; the stars paled, the first rays of the sun touched the peak of the Matterhorn which seemed to be quite near us. Then the bright sun rose and its rays fell on the glittering snow and ice. The final climb was steep and strenuous. Then, before we reached the summit, we had to cross a long narrow bridge which was just wide enough to take both feet side by side; the ground fell away steeply to right and left. At first the sight frightened me, but I did not feel dizzy; then I kept my eyes on the footsteps of the guide who, roped to me, went ahead. I stepped in his footprints and looked neither to left nor right and thus I managed quite well. From the top we had a view which surpassed description. It seemed to me as if we could see all the peaks of the Alps lying far below us. To the south we looked down to the Italian plain. I could not stay longer than perhaps 10 minutes at the top because the guide wanted to start off again. We had to be back at the hut before mid-day, because the sun became hot and melted ice and snow so that there was danger of the bridges over the glacier crevasses becoming weak. Our return was without incident but of course I arrived back at Zermatt very tired. The unforgettable highlight of this tour was the climb over the glacier under the star-filled sky above us and the following sunrise. The view from a four thousand metre peak in the Alps on a clear day is indescribably extensive; but from this height the other peaks, however high they may be, seem relatively low. Almost incomparably grander is the view from a 'three thousand' peak, surrounded by those of four thousand metres. Such a panorama, unique in its kind, is to be obtained from the 'Gorner Grat'. On this holiday I also climbed this peak with its remarkable view. I spent the night there at the Gorner Grat Hotel in order to experience the setting and the rising of the sun. I could never tire of looking at these beautiful mountain peaks. From the Gorner Grat one gets a particularly fine and clear view of Monte Rosa, its long ascending slope (a twelve-hour climb), the steep and dangerous north face and the beautiful 'Dufour Peak' which made a deep and unforgettable impression on me.

In those years I also learned to ski and took several courses of instruction in various places. There was one particularly enjoyable time which I spent in the Röhn mountains, not very far from Frankfurt, one winter when the snow was plentiful. I was one week in Gersfeld and the proprietor of the hotel recommended me a young man, Herrn Bübchen, who (against payment, of course) took me on daily tours. The highlight was our excursion to the 'Wasserkuppe'. My guide was accompanied by his girl friend. The Wasserkuppe, 950 metres high, is the highest peak in the Röhn. Even in those times there was a gliding school there, for glider pilots. The descent was long and lovely and we came down through the cold air at such a speed that at the end the tears ran down my cheeks.

As swimming and water gave me so much pleasure I spent much leisure time during those years on the water. I had become friendly with a technical assistant whose husband was very fond of sports. These pleasant people named Printz, were enthusiastic canoers. They persuaded me together with Dr Nikolaus Leitner, our then medical assistant, to purchase a folding canoe. My friendship with Nikolaus lasted through our lives and is still as warm as ever. But how should I explain this newly planned enterprise to my mother who was so prone to worry? Herr Printz and Nikolaus visited her together and promised to look after me like my own brothers and this calmed her fears. Now on Sundays we had splendid excursions on various rivers, usually with two and sometimes three boats. We often went to the 'Old Rhein', a part of the river no longer used by the main stream; it was a quiet romantic backwater. Often we paddled on the Main, from Aschaffenburg to Hanau and from there to Frankfurt. Sometimes we were also on the Neckar and the Kinzig. The boat was collapsed an evening in advance and early on Sunday morning at five or six o'clock taken on a trolly to the station. We travelled by train in the upstream direction, and built up the canoe at the starting point, for it had been taken to pieces for the transport. We generally paddled leisurely downstream. The amount of energy required for the paddling depended on the height of the river and the waterflow. We rested at a pleasant spot, swam and picnicked there. A great deal could be carried in the canoe; in addition to the two paddlers there was equipment for making coffee, drinking water, milk and sandwiches etc. In this way we were quite independent of restaurants. Once on a trip on the Rhine the men brought bottles of Niersteiner Goldberg (one bottle for each boat) on board. After we had imbibed this lovely drink I was greatly teased and it was maintained that I could no longer count the geese which we met in quite large numbers! In spring there was often high water on the Main and quite a strong current. Then the weirs which ordinarily held back the flow, were opened and we could be carried along by the rushing stream without any exertion on our part. When the weirs were closed we usually passed through the raft channels which were used by the timber rafts which could not get through the weirs. Then we unloaded all our goods and carried them overland to the other side of the weir. We put on our swim suits and navigated the boat through the raft channel in which of course the current was very strong. At the end of this

Bacteriologist in Frankfurt

channel where it entered the main stream a fairly strong counter-current formed and a small boat was in danger of capsizing. However we were all swimmers! This spice of danger increased the pleasure. In fact we never capsized.

From these descriptions it would almost seem that during my years as a bacteriologist in Frankfurt sport was my main pre-occupation. But this was certainly not so. Only holidays and Sundays were employed in this way and sport provided a good balance for the long hours of work. I worked eagerly in these years and with great satisfaction and pleasure. I qualified in 1930 as a lecturer in bacteriology in the medical faculty. After acceptance of my 'Habilitationsschrift' entitled: 'Bacterial pleomorphism and developmental processes in bacteria' I had to give a lecture before the professors of the medical faculty. This event had to be preceded by a visit to each of the professors. When I visited Professor Herxheimer, the dermatologist, he said, "You aren't afraid of the lecture? Imagine you are standing before a row of cabbages". After the lecture the professors put questions, which the candidate had to answer. Everything went very well. As I came out of the faculty assembly, the chief slipped quickly out through the rear exit, gave me his hand and said, "You have done very well". I thought, he gives twice who gives quickly. This was typical of Professor Neisser; the next day I would not have appreciated it so much. A little later a public inaugural lecture had to be given to which members of the faculty, especially the 'dekan', came, and to which relations and friends received a formal printed invitation. For this occasion I had a very attractive brown silk dress made, which, as was the fashion at the time, was longer at the back than in the front. In the evening we had a small party at home for which we provided a very good fruit cup. My inaugural lecture was printed, under the title 'Invisible life' in the journal of the Senckenberg Society *Natur und Museum*. The editors repeated at the top of the paper the words which Professor Bordet, director of the Pasteur Institute in Belgium, pronounced on the 22nd July 1930 at Pasteur's laboratory in Paris, when opening the First International Congress of Microbiology: "When Pasteur and Koch published their memorable discoveries for the good of their people and the good of all mankind, a quiver of hope spread through the whole world transcending all national boundaries which science does not recognize and which it alone one day will be able to remove". Since then 43 years have passed; we have had a second terrible and destructive world war. Atom bombs have been discovered. Nuclear weapons can be set in motion with the pressure of a single finger on a button and they could destroy half of humanity. We have made unthought-of technical progress; yet in Berlin a high wall separates the East from the West and *we* have lost our illusions: rightly or wrongly, who knows?

From 1930 on I gave lectures in Bacteriology to scientists. Beside this, the chief made me his collaborator in the course of bacteriology for medical students, in which we gave lectures alternately. He also sometimes asked me to deputize for him in the lectures for medical students, if it was the occasion for a bacteriological subject rather than one on hygiene. All this gave me great pleasure. I had already become a member of the German Society for Hygiene and Bacteriology and also attended our congresses. The last one I attended was in Giessen and I particularly remember papers by Professor Uhlenhuth from Munich and Professor Sachs from Heidelberg. Also at that time the strange 'Pettenkoferien course' was given by Professor Philaletes Kuhn in Giessen in 1931. He showed us the swollen forms of bacteria produced by lithium chloride, which he believed to be protozoa and parasites of bacteria and which he named 'Pettenkoferia' in remembrance of the famous bacteriologist Pettenkofer. He also believed in the change of one kind of bacterium into another. He gave us a culture of *Bacterium coli* which we had to put into a weak solution of phenol; after this treatment we were able to cultivate enterococci from it. The course lasted 14 days. I went back to Frankfurt for the first weekend. I took the coli culture with me and streaked it at various dilutions over a dozen plates in my laboratory. On the next day I found that a small number of colonies of enterococci had grown up from the diluted culture. This proved that the enterococci had already been present as contaminants in the original coli culture, as I had suspected. The coli bacteria were more sensitive to phenol than the enterococci and this had determined the results of our tests. On the last Saturday of the course there was a discussion. I asked Professor Kuhn if he would not prefer my not attending the discussion, as I would express my opinion freely. He said he wanted me to attend. Of course, I then said what I thought. At the close of the course there was a social occasion. As a result of my antagonistic attitude I was, so to speak, sent to Coventry. None of the men paid any attention to me or danced with me except a young Swiss, Dr Hans Schmidt and a Dutchman, Dr Postmus. Both were nice to me and visited me on their return journey, at Frankfurt. Another of the participants in the course who declared himself my friend was Baron Axel von Klinckowström, of Stockholm. He was an old gentleman of 60 years, with the largest and most splendid white beard I have ever seen. We had

Bacteriologist in Frankfurt

already corresponded before we met at Giessen about a scientific diversion over the publications of Enderlein in Berlin, who had described mitoses and similar phenomena in bacteria and illustrated them at a magnification of 20 000 times, and the electron microscope had not yet been invented in those days! When Klinckowström saw me, he said, "I thought you were an ugly old hag!" I replied, "And I thought you were a dashing young man!" From that time Klinckan, as his friends called him, was a true friend. In Giessen I lost an antique pendant and put an advertisement in the local paper; the next day the pendant was returned. When I told this to Klinckowström he said, "How could you ever lose a (de)pendant!" Ever afterwards he used to sign himself on all his letters to me as: Your old true "dependant". In his youth he had undertaken research trips round the world and collected material for museums. Later bacteriology became his hobby-horse; he had his well equipped private laboratory on his estate near Stockholm and left the management of his property to his wife. He made painstaking investigations which he illustrated with good drawings. Up to his death in 1936 I received frequent letters from him and in 1935 he invited me to Stockholm; unfortunately I became ill in Copenhagen where I was spending a few weeks in the laboratory of Dr Oerskov and could not make the journey to Stockholm. Later I shall have more to say about Klinckowström's letters. Most of them were sent to London; I have still to relate of the time which made me leave Germany and to emigrate to England.

CHAPTER V

Germany during the Rise of the Nazis

Violence can only be concealed by the lie, and the lie can be maintained only by violence.

Alexander Solzhenitsyn: Nobel Prize speech

IF ONE HAS ENJOYED throughout one's youth and almost into middle age a happy family life and if one thinks back with pleasure and love on one's parents, brothers and sister, then it is difficult to write about things which have torn the family apart and which have affected it cruelly and destroyed its members for no faults of theirs. But I have undertaken to write factually about the Hitler period and so I shall carry out this intention.

It was clear to us in 1932 that some sinister and threatening movement was afoot. Anti-Semitism grew; at the ski course anti-Semitic jokes were being told. Sometimes a column of Brownshirts marched through one of the streets of our neighbourhood while my mother and I were out of doors. Then I would pull her quickly round the corner into the next street so that we would not meet this disagreeable marching mob. In 1933 Hitler ousted the old President Hindenburg from the saddle and usurped after his death the post of Chancellor of the Realm, and he overwhelmed the German people by seizing power. Germany was then very poor and in a situation of crisis and Hitler had numerous followers who believed that everything would now be better, that unemployment would be cured and that the Germans would again become a mighty people. In the year 1934 the old and weakened Hindenburg died and Hitler was now sole Head of the State and in absolute power, supported by his Brown- and Blackshirts and the Gestapo (*Geheime Staatspolizei*, secret police).

The anti-Jewish laws came out on 28th of March 1933. As published in 'the Documents of the History of the Frankfurt Jews' (commissioned for research into the history of the Frankfurt Jews, 1933) my chief, Professor Neisser, wrote the following letter to the 'Personaldezernent' on 29.3.1933:

> On the basis of the Decree No. 103 of 28th March I find it necessary, in order to clarify my own position, to state the following:
> By race I am wholly Jewish, in my belief Protestant. But I am, above all, German and this cannot be contested by any personage of whatever rank. On my father's side and my mother's side our families have lived in Germany for centuries. I have fulfilled my duties of military service in peacetime and was in the war for four years, two of them in an operational area. The commanding General of the Prussian Guards conferred on me the Iron Cross, 1st Class and the Franz Josefs Order Knight's Cross. Before the war I became professor and holder of the R.A.O.4* and obtained during the war the title of 'Geheimer Medizinalrat'. After the war I experienced no advancement except that in 1921/22 I was entrusted with the Rectorship of the University by the Senate. I founded the Municipal Hygiene Institute in 1909, being its director from that time. Since in all the pronouncements and public notices not the denomination but the race is taken as criterion I declare myself to come under this decree and request leave of absence immediately. However my activities as professor and occupant of a chair for hygiene and bacteriology I do not surrender. Release from this must come from another side.

When this happened I had just returned from a skiing holiday and found the Institute orphaned, robbed of its guardian head. The chief still came a few times to supervise the packing of his personal belongings, his library, etc. On one occasion he returned one evening to his rooms with his wife. They had just returned from a visit to Professor Sachs in Heidelberg with whom the chief had been very friendly since their time together as pupils of Paul Ehrlich. Mrs Neisser sat down dejectedly and said, "Everything is finished." This cut me to the heart. Soon afterwards

---

* R.A.O. = Roter Adler Order.

the Neissers travelled to Switzerland, to the Pension Bellevue in Montagnola. I wrote my erstwhile chief a letter of thanks for everything he represented for me. On 9th May, 1933 he wrote me an answering letter which made me very happy, and is one of the most beautiful letters which I have ever received. I quote it in full, not only because it gave me so much pleasure but also because it shows how little we all imagined what the future would be after Hitler's accession to power.

Today we know how brutal, cruel and sadistic man can be. But *we*—let us admit it—who had been, so-to-speak, brought up in the Schiller and Goethe tradition had at that time not the faintest idea of all that man is able to inflict on man. Here now is Neisser's letter:

My dear Miss Klieneberger,
(I should really have written "Dr Kl."), it is only today that I have the opportunity to reply to your dear letter of the 4th, because we have fetched our son Gerhard from the ship in Genoa and we had so much to chat about with him. Your letter gave me (and also my wife) great pleasure and I thank you sincerely for your friendly sentiments and their expression. For many reasons I appreciate your letter particularly, since for you—as you now see—I have apparently done nothing, even though I have tried to. If you, despite the abrupt and nasty break in your career, can look back without bitterness but even with friendliness, this shows the mildness of your heart coupled with great strength of character. For us men a gloomy future so easily overshadows a pleasant and sunlit past. In the more optimistic nature of woman it is frequently very different. I would be very happy for you and also for me, if this were also to be so with you in the future. Now I must and want to thank you; this is not to be one of those numerous testimonials, which I have furnished for our pupils (to make them blush!) but the simple expression of my sincerest thanks for your faithful, understanding collaboration, for your sensitive readiness to help and forbear with a chief, who as a human being has moods and emotions and who always tried to impose his opinions. And if, in all the 10 or 11 years we never quarrelled, never have had a serious difference of opinion, this was entirely due to you. They were 10 fruitful years, 10 years of unusually harmonious collaboration and yet we saw each other usually twice, sometimes more often per day and had consultations together. This scientific understanding is unthinkable without human understanding. That existed between us and cannot be destroyed. In this sense we do not have to part. What the position will be from the scientific viewpoint

is still uncertain to me. Naturally I was very interested in your communication on the megatherium phage and your intention to investigate its effect on spore formation. Yet I almost fear this my interest now. For this interest rouses questions. But what is the use of questions if I have no longer the possibility to get close to the answers by my own endeavours. Nevertheless I think it is the right thing for you to turn your attention to the more scientific and not medical aspect of our subject. (Of course, at once a subsidiary question. Has our dextrorotatory megatherium organism spores? Does one see in their arrangement any signs of growth in right turns?)

Well my dear Dr Klieneberger, at the moment I have no intention of leaving Frankfurt. So perhaps we will with congenial people arrange a kind of discussion group at some evening or something similar and in any case we will not allow our good relationships and our harmonious human and scientific associations to perish.

I send you my sincere greetings and those of my wife. My greetings also to your mother.

As always, M. Neisser.

How clearly one sees from this letter that Professor Neisser thought that elderly people, who had been dismissed from their posts, because of the 'Aryan Clause' could live peacefully—although in a backwater—on their personal incomes and pensions. No one dreamed that these good citizens would one day be fetched by the Nazi police, put into concentration camps and, finally, end their lives in the gas chambers. We survivors cannot be reproached because our imagination could not encompass this, although I never feel quite free of guilt. If we had had any intimation we could well have saved one or the other of these people before it was too late. The younger people who during the year 1933 were dismissed from their posts or lost their opportunities to work, naturally told themselves that they had still many years of work before them and that emigration was the only solution for themselves. In 1933 it was still easy to leave Germany. One could obtain a German passport without difficulty and travel to a foreign country. This raised no special obstacles, especially if one could hope to find work there. Many countries such as England and America showed themselves generous at that time in accepting immigrants. But the plight of the older people was frightful! Professor Neisser died of a heart attack in 1938 and his wife, who was born in America, could again take on her American citizenship. She returned to New York but unfortunately died in 1939 of cancer of the spinal marrow.

By their early demise these two fine persons did not have to experience the worst fates which faced many like them. My brother-in-law, Julius, so rightly said of the Nazis, "They draw back one curtain after another!" And so it was, and each curtain hid a still more dreadful image. At first it was believed that the old people would be left in peace and it was made known that Jewish men who had fought and distinguished themselves in the First World War would not be affected. This applied to my two brothers; and so I believed them to be safe. This proved later to be a misconception. I myself, after the dismissal of my good chief, worked sadly on at the Institute. We received a new director, not a bad man but a nonentity. He knew hardly any bacteriology and often before his lectures he put simple questions to me as a preparation for these.

Altogether it was not uninteresting to see how the chaff separated from the grain. All my close Aryan friends remained true; I was not deceived in any of those. But more superficial acquaintances sometimes behaved differently; they trimmed their sails to the wind. A botanist, an assistant professor, who had several times invited me to his house, had the effrontery to say to me, "If I had known you were of Jewish descent I would have had nothing to do with you". Shortly before he had paid me attention, because he wanted to be appointed to the chair and thought I could put in a good word with my chief, who was considered an influential person. One saw here and there people slide into posts for which they were quite unsuited; merely because they belonged to the party while decent people were reserved and withdrew. To my great disgust I one day saw the photograph of my dear Professor Möbius (pure 'Aryan') in *Der Stürmer*, the dreadful Nazi paper, which hung at every street corner, specially protected in a glass case. The picture illustrated an article attacking him fiercely; for the courageous old gentleman had dared to attack the authorities for dismissing Jewish members of the university, pointing out that the university owed its existence largely to Jewish endowment. The dear old couple, Professor Möbius and his wife, retreated completely to Bad Homburg during the Nazi period and remained to the last good friends to my sister there.

In the first weeks of the Hitler regime I would gladly have left the country at once. My work was the greatest factor in my life and I was just 40 years old; and I knew there were no further possibilities for me in Germany. Yet the Association of University Women advised me not to leave before I was dismissed lest people abroad should not believe that I could no longer practise my profession in Germany. For consultation with older members of this Association I went in the spring of 1933 for a

Germany during the Rise of the Nazis

week to Berlin, where I also visited my friend Nikolaus Leitner for the last time before our emigration. We next met 27 years later, in Geneva. We had both experienced much in the meantime: Nikolaus, who came from good Hungarian-Jewish stock, soon after my visit in Berlin went to Bucharest. His home-town, Grosswardein in Hungary, became Romanian after the First World War and so he also inevitably became Romanian. He started a practice in the Romanian capital which soon flourished, as he was a very capable doctor. When the Nazis came to Romania he was put in a concentration camp where he played the role of a doctor as far as possible. He survived the war and returned to Bucharest where meanwhile the communists had taken over control. Private practice was no longer possible and he had to accept, as a state-employed doctor, a badly paid post and could no longer practise his medical profession in accordance with his own conscience and knowledge. After he had endured this depressing state of affairs up to 1960, he succeeded, after overcoming incredible difficulties, in emigrating legally, on condition of leaving behind all his possessions. He could not even take his gold wrist watch along; he had to exchange it for a steel one. He first went to Geneva, where his elder brother lived, who had been given asylum by the Swiss because he and his family had survived a concentration camp and above all because he had money abroad and was not destitute. In Geneva I met Nikolaus again and heard his story; from Geneva he went to Israel where he has since been working as a doctor and in 1960 at the age of 56 had to start again. We can now correspond openly and continue to be good friends. I have never heard a word of complaint from him. He knows no bitterness and has preserved that same serious-gay charming manner which he had in his youth.

Now back to myself. I kept going at the Frankfurt Institute of Hygiene until the end of June 1933. Then it occurred to me that I had six weeks holiday due to me, which I on no account wished to give to the City of Frankfurt, my employer. So I took leave and stayed at home. In mid-August I received a note from the City in which I was informed that I—without pension—was relieved of my duties and that I was forbidden to visit my place of employment with the intention of contesting this judgement. I was then allowed to go there once more to fetch my books and notes. The kind employee of the Institute, Pfister, who prepared our culture media, socialist and very anti-Nazi in his good soul got himself a handcart and together with his young son brought all my books and other belongings to my home. With the mentioned 'chit' from the municipal authorities I went to see Professor Neisser. He said only: "Is that the reward for faithful services?" He gave me his friendship and his warm interest to the end of his days. He was a great personality to whom the city of Frankfurt owed a lot. However, at the time of his death no obituary appeared either in the German scientific journals or in the newspapers. I asked my new director, Sir John C.G. Ledingham, to write his obituary for an English journal. He wrote a dignified article that was published in the *Lancet* * of the same year. In order to express the thanks I owed to him I wrote an article about his contributions to bacteriology and hygiene in remembrance of his 100th birthday in 1969.[†] After his untimely retirement in spring 1933 he retreated to his holiday house at Falkenstein in the Taunus mountains. His interest in his friends and pupils never faltered. Although bedridden some weeks before his death he still wrote to me about his great interest in my work. He died on 25th February 1938 in complete ignorance of all the sufferings inflicted on the Jewish people in the forthcoming years.

He said in an article that it was the greatest luck of his scientific life that he worked under Flügge and Ehrlich. I am in a similar way grateful for having been able to work for eleven years under his guidance.

---

* *Lancet*, March 12, 1938.
† *Zbl. Bakt. I. Abt. Orig.* **215** (1970) p. 279.
See also: *Schweizerische Med. Wo.schr.* **68,** Jahrgang 1938 Nr 20, S.566 (Hans Sachs).

CHAPTER VI

Life and Work in England

DURING THE LAST few months in Germany I had written all sorts of letters abroad, in a sense putting out feelers all round. One letter I had even sent to the famous Professor Landsteiner who was working in the Rockefeller Institute in New York. He replied very amiably to me and said that he could not promise anything at that distance, but if only I were in the U.S.A. the situation might well be different. I inferred from this that I would have had opportunities in the U.S.A. Today I'm sure I would have made good progress there. What I did not imagine was that from there I could probably have saved my mother and sister, especially as America entered the war much later than England. But who could foresee these events? It is not given to any of us to see into the future. England especially attracted me and it was the country of my choice. A particular motive for this was that I remained near to my family, especially my mother and could easily and frequently visit her from there, which I did up to 1938. So London was my goal. In the next fortnight I provided myself with new clothing and linen. Then I packed a small suitcase and travelled on the night train to Ostend with my friend Liesel, who also wanted to look for employment in London. My dear sister accompanied us to the train. Parting was a little sad, for one rarely travels cheerfully into uncertainty in the night. Acquaintances in Frankfurt had recommended me a guest house in Kensington and they had reserved a room for me. My first London experience was that the taxi driver swindled me and gave me too little change out of my good pound sterling. However in the guest house I was accommodated well, reasonably, if rather simply. I knew not a single person in London, nor in the whole of England. But a young chemist of my acquaintance had met a young English bacteriologist, Dr B.C.J.G. Knight at a conference. He gave me a recommendation to this young man who was then assistant to Sir Paul Fildes. I wrote to him and visited him at the Institute for Medical Research in Hampstead. He said it was useless for us to approach Dr Fildes for he was anti-Irish and anti-Semitic and that the Lister Institute in Chelsea, on the other hand, should be considered. He told me to write to Dr Felix, who of course was known to me as the discoverer together with Weil of the Weil-Felix reaction used all over the world for the diagnosis of typhus. I wrote to Dr Felix and visited him at the Lister Institute. Dr Felix was an extremely cautious man, which should not be taken as a reproach, for later as my colleague he was very good to me. So instead of introducing me to the director, Dr J.C.G. Ledingham, or asking him if he wished to see me, he referred me to the then already existing Academic Assistance Council and said I should request the council to give me a letter of introduction to Dr Ledingham. I sent this off and Dr Ledingham requested me to visit him at the Lister Institute. He conversed with me for nearly an hour, in English, of course. I had no intimation that he had spent a year in Leipzig and that at that time his German was much better than my English. I had requested not a post but working accommodation, because at that time, 200 M a month could still be sent from Germany. It was my greatest wish to be allowed to work in a bacteriological laboratory again. Whether or not I used up my German savings was all one to me at that time. Dr Ledingham dismissed me with the information that he would ask the 'Governing Body' whether I could have a work bench in the Institute. Also at that time Professor Neisser happened to be in London for the wedding of his son which was celebrated there. So Dr Ledingham said "send me your former chief". I said, "I cannot send him but I will ask him to visit you." Shortly afterwards I received a few lines from Dr Ledingham informing me that on the first of October I could begin my work at the Lister Institute. He proposed I should occupy myself with the causative organisms of pleuropneumonia in cattle and agalactia in sheep. Since this was quite a new field for me, I gladly undertook it, because everything new greatly stimulated me. I had been just a fortnight in London when I began to work in the Lister Institute and I had enquired only there and nowhere else. That I would continue to work there for the rest of my working life (exactly 29 years) I could not foresee then.

The first free fortnight I had I used in looking around London. I was completely fascinated and charmed by the giant city in which one could, nevertheless, easily find one's way. I used no public transport but only walked. I saw the parks, which in this warm and sunny September (we had an 'Indian summer') showed their most beautiful aspect. I found it wonderful to be in London—'the hub of the world'; I visited the museums, the Tower of London; I stood on Westminster Bridge and saw St Paul's Cathedral. I was completely enthralled. On October 1st when I began my work, I moved to Crosby Hall, the club of the British Federation of University Women. I obtained a small room there and I felt at ease in that atmosphere. It was good to be in completely British surroundings and also good for progress with the language, which I wanted as far as possible to master. Moreover Crosby Hall was in the neighbourhood of the Lister Institute so that I could walk between the two.

Many people think that my dismissal and 'enforced emigration' were cruel. Of course, the dismissal, coming out of the blue, was a momentary shock and I was almost more shocked by the removal of my good chief. The immigration itself, the achieving of a foothold in a new highly civilized country, the learning of a new language, the adaptation to another culture, were a great and satisfying enrichment for me; I was 40 years old, had already achieved something in my profession, had amassed some experience, had seen a little of the world but was still young enough to absorb novelty with avidity.

How wonderful would it be if all national boundaries were opened and we could move freely from one country into another. Could we at last give up the restrictions of 'nationalism' and not be satisfied with 'United Nations' or 'Internationalism' and instead become 'Supernationalists?' However, we re-arm continually for so-called reasons of defence and produce arms which at any time may be used and probably will be used for mutual destruction. We should adopt Beethoven's wonderful message: "All men become brothers" as our leading motive. The means for the carrying out of this message are in our hands! It would not only make us much richer in a spiritual sense but also be of tremendous material advantage. The enormous amounts of money and resources we spend on armament could be used for better purposes, for housing, education, help for the underdeveloped countries and many other things. It seems this to be such an obvious idea, but it always escapes our grasp like a Fata Morgana.

My life in two different countries such as Germany and England was for me a great spiritual enrichment for which I am very grateful. A pity only that such an unlucky political situation was its cause.

However, right in the beginning I had the good fortune both in the Lister Institute and in Crosby Hall, to enter into an intellectual environment which greatly appealed to me. In my work I felt I had passed from one pair of good hands (Neisser's) into another pair (Ledingham's). At first Dr Ledingham frequently came into my laboratory. He looked into my records; apparently he wished to see in which language they were written. Naturally from the very first day they were in English. Suddenly Dr Ledingham stopped coming; I asked Dr Felix whether this was a bad sign. "On the contrary", he said, "he has seen that you need no supervision". But Dr Ledingham still came every few months to hear what I was doing and to discuss my work with me, which was always pleasant and stimulating. At his request I had already given my first demonstration at Christmas 1933 at the meeting of the Society of Pathology and Bacteriology in London and I showed my preparations of the organisms of pleuropneumonia of cattle and agalactia of sheep. I worked long hours in the laboratory with immense satisfaction and in the evenings read journals and studied the English language. I sought to make good my deficiencies in the knowledge of English classical literature. On Sunday mornings I often visited the Temple Church. There a different minister preached every Sunday and he spoke slowly in very good English. This helped me considerably; for first one learns to read a language, then to speak and write it and lastly—if at all—to understand the spoken language. I didn't speak much at first but I kept my ears open! Of course I could not lose my accent completely, or what a friend of mine politely calls 'my continental voice'. It falls to very few to eliminate this and it is not necessary to do so, for—naturally—one always remains to some extent a 'refugee', even if one is no longer, as at first, an 'alien'. No one can assimilate or integrate himself fully! This must be realized quite clearly. In Germany I would soon have been given the title of professor, and as my chief desired it, perhaps would have obtained a lectureship (*Lehrauftrag*). As a woman I would never have been appointed to a chair in Germany. In England I achieved less, but nevertheless I found a niche, a permanent post in a first-class institute and I became known in the scientific circles of my subject. I didn't earn very much (I could have if I had gone into industry; but this did not suit me). I earned less than in Germany; but I was not interested in money; what I received was quite sufficient for my needs. In respect of human relations I could be well satisfied. I was gradually accepted by my circle of colleagues as one of them and I did not lack friends. What more could I have desired? It exceeded my expectations. England is my adopted motherland and I would not like to exchange it for any other. If my family had not perished so tragically under the Nazis I could be completely happy to the end of my days in England. But of course this cannot and should not be forgotten, and even if subconsciously, it is always there in the background of my mind. Of course I often forget about it, yet that is quite right, for if one wishes to live on after such events (and I wished to!) one must lead a normal life.

Back once again to the events of the years preceding the war. In 1934 my first English paper was published in the *Journal of Pathology and Bacteriology* under the title: 'The colonial development of the organism of pleuropneumonia and agalactia. . .'. Of course the style was corrected by Dr Ledingham. Afterwards the idea came to me that there probably were more such strange organisms which were similar to each other but different from bacteria and all other organisms I knew. I began to search systematically for such organisms. Dr Ledingham was not taken with this idea; he said that he was quite pleased that there were already two such organisms. However he let me continue. I thought one should search on mucous membranes and began my first search with guinea-pigs. I was unsuccessful there! Next I continued my exploratory research with rats and mice. I had prepared a very good nutrient medium which was suitable for culturing the organisms of pleuropneumonia and agalactia. The rats of the Lister Institute and all other breeds generally suffered from a strange bronchopneumonia, first indicated by hepatization of some lung lobes; then lesions formed which on cutting open released a purulent fluid and finally lung abscesses were formed which contained a cheese-like mass. No one so far had been able to cultivate from these lung lesions a microbe which could have been regarded as the etiological cause of the disease. One day when I had smeared culture plates of my medium with the pus from these abscesses I found that after two to three days of incubation minute colonies had grown up on my plates similar in appearance to those of the organisms of pleuropneumonia and agalactia. The lungs of all these diseased rats were thus infected and I described these organisms as pleuropneumonia-like. Dr Ledingham was astonished! Consequently I found a number of similar organisms in rats and mice, even in wild rats, which the rat catcher brought to me alive. These microbes were the causes of various diseases in these rodents which I studied in those years. I got together a collection of pleuropneumonia-like organisms (PPLO), now Mycoplasmas, which I maintained in pure culture on small plates for many years. My discoveries gave me great pleasure and I sometimes woke in the middle of the night with excitement as to what my cultures would show the next day.

In many respects I was well equipped for my work. At that time the Lister Institute provided neither microscopes nor photographic equipment for its research workers. In olden times it was almost exclusively those people with private means who devoted themselves to scientific research in England. The deficiency of the Lister Institute was probably a survival of that time and the Lister workers all possessed their own microscopes, though usually not of the best quality. At the beginning of 1934 I returned to Frankfurt to visit my mother and sister in Bad Homburg. From there I travelled to Jena where I was still very obligingly received in the Zeiss works and there I purchased a first-class research microscope with many apochromatic objectives and also a Leitz dark ground condenser which was the best made at that time. I also bought in Frankfurt a Leica camera with an adaptor for the microscope and enlarging equipment with all the necessary accessories. Of course I had to pay duty on all this optical equipment; but the English customs officers were very understanding and did not demand very much. Now I could illustrate all my papers with my own photographs and I was also certain of possessing the best possible working tools of the time. At this time I came across an organism called *Streptobacillus moniliformis*; I was surprised at the many soft forms which occurred in it. After some endeavour I succeeded finally in producing a pure culture of these soft forms which seemed to have no cell walls and grew well on my special medium. I was able to maintain them in pure culture in indefinite passages and had thus isolated the first stable L-phase of a bacterium. I chose the letter L for this peculiar phase because I had bred it in the Lister Institute. This designation has now become entrenched in the literature. At that time my investigations were regarded as curiosities without importance. This did not worry me and I was firmly convinced that the world could not always pass over these researches without noticing their importance. When I first reported on *Streptobacillus moniliformis* and its L-phase at a meeting in London, Dr Gardner strongly opposed my view; he did not believe that the L-phase was stable. I defended my position and heard someone behind me say, "She sticks to her guns". Naturally it was particularly important to me that Dr Ledingham should find my investigations interesting and noteworthy. He described my studies in an Annual Report of the Lister Institute as pioneer work and reported on it in a lecture which he gave in America.

Life and Work in England

Another director might have said, "Stop this nonsense which is of interest to no-one and do something more realistic". Not so Dr Ledingham! He was a very clever and also a very kind man and he had a charming family. At that time the director and his family still lived in the flat in the upper storey of the Institute. Sometimes Mrs Ledingham invited a few of us women for tea at 4.30; Dr Ledingham joined us and we spent a pleasant hour with this charming couple. I also spent many a Christmas Day with the director's family. He regularly invited people at Christmas who were alone or had no real Christmas at home. Of course there was good English Christmas fare, and Jack, the growing son of the house, served us neatly and skilfully. Toasts were drunk, "To our kith and kin; to our friends far and near" and finally, "To our noble selves". Usually the Felixes, Dr Petrie, the director of our branch institute at Elstree, and I were present. Those were unforgettable happy occasions. Usually we stayed to tea and only returned home in the late afternoon.

A few months after I started to work in England the sending of money from Germany was forbidden by the Nazis. But university women in England had collected money to help their German emigré colleagues. The money sufficed for three grants which consisted of accommodation and free board at Crosby Hall. I was one of the three women selected to benefit from this. At this time I had also applied for a normal scholarship which the International Federation of University Women donated annually. Professor Johanna Westerdyck, from Baarn in Holland, a very well-known botanist and Director of the Institute for Mould Cultures, interviewed me. I found her very sympathetic and was very pleased to meet her again some years later. Yet at that time she said to me, "Should you obtain the scholarship don't remain at the Lister Institute, you will never get on there". I obtained the scholarship and continued to work at the Lister Institute because I liked it there, and I didn't want to put the Atlantic Ocean between me and my family. But now I had simultaneously two grants, the Residential Scholarship at Crosby Hall and £305 from the International Federation of University Women. I went to the warden of Crosby Hall, Miss Spurling, a charming elderly lady. I expressed to her my doubts. She said, "It is all right, we have given you the Residential Scholarship and the other you have received for your brains". That was very pleasing. As my scholarship year was coming to an end I heard from someone of a post for a bacteriologist at Glaxo, one of the large English pharmaceutical firms; I spoke with one of their people. He said I should apply, so I wrote an application and collected together papers, testimonials, etc. But before I sent anything off, I went to Dr Ledingham, showed him everything and asked him if I should apply. He merely said, "If you want to make money, my answer is 'yes'; otherwise you are not a problem". I didn't send my application; he had mislaid it and never returned it to me. I now knew Dr Ledingham very well; if he only gave a slight hint, this was more than ten promises from another man or the irrevocable contracts which I had from the City of Frankfurt. Somewhat later Dr Ledingham, still in coat, hat and with his umbrella, came into my laboratory to tell me that the Lister Institute had granted me the Jenner Memorial Scholarship for three years. Of course Dr Ledingham had known that his proposal carried final weight with the Governing Body. But he had not said a word about it until it was signed and sealed. I could now continue my work to my heart's content.

Meanwhile a few other people had started to work in my field. Dr Louis Dienes in Boston occupied himself with L-phases and PPLO. We corresponded and met at the International Congress for Microbiology in London in 1936. Dr Ørskov from Copenhagen also came at that time and was interested in the subject. In Tokyo a Dr Shoetensack cultivated PPLO strains from dogs. In London, Dr Laidlaw and Dr Elford found the saprophytic strains which are present in sewage and soil. I was in contact with all these people and received cultures from them. At one of our meetings I also became acquainted with Dr Peyton Rous. A young man, Dr Smith, who had worked with Dienes, was Rous's assistant and had aroused the chief's interest in the L-phases. Dr Rous invited me to a cup of coffee and conversed with me in a very agreeable manner. I have never forgotten the attention this famous man showed me nor the charming old gentleman himself. In the summer of 1935 I spent three weeks in the Serum Institute in Copenhagen in Dr Ørskov's laboratory. These were pleasant weeks—especially on account of Dr Ørskov's friendliness—but he and I did not quite agree on the morphology of the PPLO and L-phases and after that we did not get on quite as well when we met at conferences.

It is remarkable how many short moments of one's life impress themselves deeply on the memory. Professor Albert Einstein came to London and also visited the Lister Institute. Dr Ledingham introduced me to him. He shook hands with me and still today I can see before me Professor Einstein's intelligent face with its soft and kind features.

In those years before the Second World War many kind and interesting letters were sent to me from abroad. I have already mentioned the Baron Dr Axel von Klinckowström. His letters pleased me greatly. He was famous in his fatherland Sweden as an explorer and as an author of many

Life and Work in England

widely read books. He was also a bacteriologist and very interested in my work. Here follow parts of his charming letters:

Stafsund, 30.4.1935
My dear lady!

At last I have some time to write letters! The proofs for my summer novel are fortunately completed, the illustrations for the fourth part of my memoirs are assembled and are now being photographed, so at last I have some freedom for letter writing and also something to recount about Fräulein Margarethe Zülzer and her reception at the Microbiological Society here in this country. Fräulein Z. was a very imposing personality, as tall as I am, built like a Valkyrie, red-haired with a large hooked nose. Age 50 to 60. Otherwise quite pleasant and with 'the gift of the gab'. On the first day Kling gave an excellent lunch in her honour in the Opernkeller, to which gastronomic occasion were invited, apart from Fräulein Z., Professor Alfred Pettersen with wife, Professor Henschen and my modest self. The next day a meeting at the Microbiological Society, with a paper by Margarethe Zülzer on the biology and epidemiology of Weil's disease—excellent!—After the public transactions there was a communal dinner in the Rosenbad restaurant with over 50 people at table. All very merry and I arrived home only at half-past one! Next day I collected Frl. Zülzer at her hotel and drove her to Stafsund for lunch, Kling and his assistant also being present. They all drove late at night to the town and the following day Frl. Zülzer was invited by the Henschens. I have the impression that the good lady was well pleased with her reception. Naturally I spoke of you, greatly esteemed, and your discoveries. To my by no means slight annoyance the Zülzer seemed very sceptical about this. She asserted that in Copenhagen—she was currently working there with Madsen—it was the opinion that your filamentary nets were not living material but *decomposition material* and so more or less artifacts! Naturally I defended you and your viewpoint with tooth and nail, without much success. Margarethe Zülzer does not seem to me to belong to those people who are easily converted.

Stafsund, 25.6.1935
Dear lady!

This time I'm really ashamed that you had to wait so long for an answer to your last two kind letters. It's just that I have been busy with a new literary 'crime'—a new novel—as I feared, even said, is *dreadful trash*: takes place in the year 1955 with stratospheric aviators, television, etc. Whether I can persuade my conservative Jewish publisher Bonnier to print it seems dubious to me! Yet once I have an idea in my head I never let it go and so there is nothing left to me but to 'write' it out, as I have done! When I am working on such a thing I am like a capercailzie in the mating season—blind and deaf. Now however it is ready; late last night I could write 'Finis' at the end of the twenty-first chapter. Now once again I can answer letters and start with you, most appreciated lady. It is indeed a pity that you cannot, as you intended, come here at this season. Sweden is at its most beautiful with these long days, the meadows abounding in flowers and the wonderful summer heat! In September you will find it quite different. . . But when you are in Copenhagen and have made your plans, please let me know and Kling and I will see what can be done.

From another letter:

So we hope to see you here in Stockholm in June. Naturally—as far as my old poor limbs allow—I am fully at your disposal and it will be an honour and pleasure to introduce you to Kling and elsewhere. My novel is today in the bookshops and the proofs of the fourth part of my memoirs finally delivered to the publisher. So I am free from it and can again devote some time to bacteriology and see what is happening in this field. . .

From the last letter, 20.4.1936

Many thanks for your welcome letter of 12.4. There is nothing much to report about myself. I am still working on my 'Tales'. So far I have reached the early Stone Age (North Sea still dry land, bison, buffalo, sun worship, human sacrifice, dashing priestesses, etc.). One item of news I have: *I am coming to London* at the end of July to the Congress of the International Microbiological Society. I am on the Nomenclature Committee with Alfred Pettersen as a member for Sweden. To my great delight I see that you my dear lady, are on the programme to give a talk on your discoveries. So we shall once again meet there. Can you not arrange that we can sit together at the closing banquet on 31.7.1936? *That would be fine!* Pettersen and I shall travel together. I have read with great interest about your work on cancer-like diseases in rats and look forward to hearing about it when at last we meet in July. Do you know if any of our happy band in Giessen will also meet

Life and Work in England

in London? If only war, insurrection or any other uproar does not intervene!

From a letter from Frau Tyra von Klinckowström:

My husband was looking forward so much to making this journey to England in the summer. His heart was however very strained and weakened, so that perhaps he would not have had the strength to participate in a Congress. That he did not have to realize this disappointment is a consolation for me, also that he was spared a long illness and old age. He had the end he always wanted. A light was extinguished.

Also my revered old university teacher, Professor Martin Möbius, sent many charming letters to me right up to the beginning of the war. I will quote some of them in the following and I hope that these unassuming but warm documents will give an idea of this distinguished man of high integrity who has accomplished so much, who still studied and painted in advanced old age and also wrote at that a time a history of botany which was so much appreciated that only recently a new edition was published. The letters also throw some light on this period of the Nazi-regime in Germany because the old gentleman was sometimes a bit outspoken, though everybody knew that letters sent abroad were frequently opened by the Nazi officials. Anyhow, this professor was very courageous and dared to express his opinions openly, which is proved by a letter published in the same document as Neisser's letter, printed on page 71. Here it is:

A letter from Professor Dr Möbius to the Lord Mayor, 15.7.1935, published in Der Stürmer*, *under the title 'The Professor'.*

Presumably you have already seen how the Bockenheim road has been disfigured by a huge anti-Semitic poster on the fence of the Gontard house. I am convinced this was done without the consent of the Lord Mayor and that I may turn to him in all confidence.

We Frankfurters must indeed feel ashamed in front of foreigners visiting the town that here Jew-baiting is pursued in such a hateful and tasteless way, since Frankfurt has to be grateful to its Jewish citizens for a whole range of gifts and charitable foundations for the benefit of

---

* The hideous Nazi paper.

the town. I give as an example the Rothschild Library and the Georg-Speyer House and remember that Frankfurt would never have become a university town, if special Jews had not donated the necessary funds.

In the hope that my complaint will not remain the only one and its justification will be acknowledged, I request you, the Lord Mayor to act against this excessive anti-Semitism.

Der Stürmer, September 1935, No, 39, p.7.

Now my letters from Professor Möbius:

Frankfurt a. Main, 18.12.1934

Yesterday your brother-in-law visited us and said that you would not be coming at Christmas; we had looked forward to your visit. So we send you are best wishes for the festival and the close of the year with heartfelt thanks for your so appreciated letter and the kind greetings on my birthday. You said so many good things about me that I am quite embarassed; thank heavens it is just 'entre nous!' What flattering things shall I say of you when you already have such success in London! I should merely wish that they would try to secure you in some brilliant (or at least, good) position and that the British would say to the Germans, "We are happy to have the people you have thrown out"...

I received a quantity of congratulations on the 7th December, such as I had never thought possible, for people must soon be tired of congratulating me, firstly on my '70th', then my 50-year doctorate and then again my 75th birthday. It is quite another matter when one becomes 90, as did my cousin Leonore Schleiden on the 5th December. She celebrated her birthday with us... The Lord Mayor sent her and me a bunch of orchids and anthuriums. The university sent me written greetings in especially appreciative terms. Dean Laibach and Professor Dieterle came forward in person with 'Heil H.!' and a huge basket of flowers...

This afternoon one might think to be in London, it is so foggy while yesterday we enjoyed sunshine and blue skies. At a quarter to five it is so dark that I have to stop writing. So, all good wishes and our heartfelt greetings from both of us.

5.6.1937

Thank you for your welcome letter and all good wishes for your new home. Unfortunately we cannot see it for it is too difficult to come to

England. However we now wait to see whether we receive in July the currency allowance for Switzerland which we ordered in the beginning of May. I have also heard it is very difficult for you to make a visit to Germany. Is this so, or may we see you soon again? Special thanks for the beautiful coronation stamps. I had looked forward to giving them to our minister's wife from Zürich, but instead of coming she has suddenly become ill and had to postpone her visit indefinitely. So everything is still uncertain, when she comes, when and where we travel. In any case I must still be here in June to deal with the proofs, if even they are quite well advanced (up to p. 370), with fairly large, close-printed pages. My wife helps, Dr Höfer helps and yet there still remain one or more errors, to my great annoyance. I have still to add a few pages of 'Corrections' and 'Addenda'. Actually I should have read through the manuscript yet again carefully, but I had become so tired of it, and I also wanted to see it in print, one never knows what will happen to oneself or what will take place; suddenly there is no more paper, or something. . . we hear nothing of the Neissers. . . but telephoning is still possible. No doubt you are still in correspondence with him. At Whitsun we were in Heidelberg, staying once again near the entrance to the castle. Hans came on Saturday and drove with us on Monday evening. Of the huge crowds of people which went to and from the Schlossberg to the castle from early morning to evening we saw nothing from the rear of the house. Before the departure we still had a fine run in the car by way of Kohlhof and Neckargemünd and then to the station. Since then we have had mostly fine weather here also, which I enjoy best at the open window, where I have the blue skies and green trees before my eyes. Thus one becomes old. But before dinner I am still a few hours in the library. But I am concerned about what I shall begin when my book is finished. I must once again search for a literary theme. The worthy Professor Meissner (successor of Wachsmuth) already experienced how terrible it is for a scientist when he is deprived of his Institute. His wife was of the wrong 'race' and so he was suddenly dismissed. Of course it is to be hoped that he will be welcomed elsewhere, for he is recognised as an excellent scholar. . . I was greatly amused that you were pleased about the bus strike, which was represented as so terrible in the papers.

10.12.1937

Although I have not yet answered your card of 17.10.37 and the letter of 20.11.37, yet you have been so good as to write to me again on 7.12.37.

Quite moved, I must express my heartfelt thanks! When, with old age, the number of acquaintances becomes ever less, it is doubly pleasing to have such a good friend even abroad. I shall count even upon this for as long as I am allowed to live. . . We should gladly hear of your paper to the Pathology Congress in January so that we can enjoy it and be proud of our acquaintance. . . For myself, the main thing is that I have continuous work, which incites me to ever new studies in the library. For my own investigations with the microscope I no longer have the laboratory though the incentive for this often occurs. It is the same for Neisser. He is now somewhere in Italy with his wife, perhaps even in Sicily. We met the couple shortly before the journey at Herxheimer's (*Author's note: The highly respected and widely known Professor Herxheimer, in his advanced old age, was put into the concentration camp in Theresienstadt, where he died*).

31.12.1937

As we heard yesterday, you had a very interesting and pleasant Christmas. The Schönemanns were so good as to invite all three of us and your sister gave us the pleasure of reading your letter to us, which so vividly describes your experiences and gives a picture of the still romantic conditions in England. One feels transported to the time of the Vicar of Wakefield, but cannot grasp how the tradition of freezing can be so valued! And this made the greater impression on us as it has been very cold in recent days, today several degrees below zero. But we have our good central heating and never freeze even when we go from the room into the hall. Poetry is represented when—just as I rise—I see the silhouettes of the trees and of the English church raise themselves against the clear morning skies. But generally the choice is to use a substitute!

The journey to Homburg was stimulating for us, but a very pleasant stimulus. It particularly pleased us to see your mother so healthy and cheerful, she does not seem to have become any older. We hope she can celebrate her 90th birthday in such good circumstances. It was so 'gemütlich' and your letter enhanced the pleasure of our meeting. If only, however, you yourself could be present it would be still better and we look forward to that.

In 1938 I was in Germany for the last time before the war. At all restaurants and hotels there were notices, 'No Jews allowed'. It happened that German Jews who had come to Germany from abroad on a visit were held at the frontier and refused permission to leave. I visited the German Embassy in London. They issued me a permit for a fortnight's visit to Bad Homburg and in particular assured my return journey to England. At the border I had to show this paper together with my passport in which had been entered as a second name 'Sarah', which was given at that time to all Jewish women. Hitler certainly didn't know that generally this name was much liked in England and some emigrants retained it because it was so well liked. At the border I had to fill in a long form; it was a disagreeable procedure. In Homburg a policeman came twice a week to my family to see if I were still there, since I was not allowed to leave Bad Homburg to visit any other place in Germany. On the return journey, by chance, I crossed the border quite unnoticed. I sat in a compartment which was otherwise taken by an English travel agency. When the customs officers came I interpreted as the English women knew no German; the passport officer however knew no English; I was taken to be the interpreter for the travel agency and I had neither to show my passport nor any other papers. In those days one was always relieved when the border had been passed! That however was the last time I ever saw my mother and sister.

In 1938 conditions came to a climax and the position of the Jews became increasingly more difficult. My brother Carl in Zittau had to endure disgraceful impositions. He lived for his profession and under his direction the hospital had expanded and gained in reputation. As a relaxation from long hours of work he indulged in some physical exercise. He was a very good horseman and regularly attended a riding school. One day he was informed that he could no longer attend. In the mornings before seven o'clock, before starting his day's duties, he used to go regularly to swim in the public swimming baths. He was probably the only bather at this early hour. One morning the woman at the paybox informed him that his visits were no longer permitted. Yet he bore all this. But when, after his dismissal from the hospital, in autumn 1938, his licence to practise was to be withdrawn, this blow was too much for him. It meant that he had to close down his private practice and would not be allowed to see any more patients. It can only be imagined how such an upright, irreproachable, capable and highly respected man had to encounter such disgusting injuries. Probably also the thought came to him that his 'Aryan' wife and his 'half-Aryan children' could get along better without him and this may have influenced his action. In any case at that time a short letter came to me in London from my dear, courageous sister-in-law Gustel. This said:

Memoirs

My dear Emmy,

Carl left us today, after 6 o'clock, for ever. He could not endure forfeiting his licence to practice tomorrow. He was so desperately unhappy. We cannot deny him this peace. We have had fine runs in the car every day, which father enjoyed.

In this deep sorrow I embrace you, your Gustel. 30.9.1938.

In the announcement of his death it said, "His life's purpose was to care for his patients and his family". He had sent his wife, late in the afternoon, to fetch a bottle of wine from the cellar; when she returned she found him dead in his chair with a stop-watch in his hand. He had taken potassium cyanide and had probably tried to see how long he could retain consciousness. Before this act, which he performed after careful consideration, he had written farewell letters to all his close relations. To his wife he wrote:

Dear Gustel,

To remain true to one's innermost self, to look upon life philosophically, to become a sacrifice to revolution, if any other way is dishonourable and becomes insupportable, is duty's call in the darkest hours.

Your grateful Carl.

To his mother:

My dear Mama,

I know I am causing you the greatest sorrow! But your son can no longer go on living a life without relatively satisfying work and with continuous humiliation from outside. Even Julius and Annie must agree to this when they consider it factually and calmly.

With true love and the attachment of your child—Carl.

My mother, then ninety years of age, wrote to me clearly in a legible hand as follows:

My well-beloved child,

I have received your two letters of the 2nd and 3rd of this month and I thank you for your *great affection*. There is no consolation for our great loss; we have to remain calm and live on with our most sincere memories of our dear Carl, who was such a joy to his father and to me during his lifetime and was always the best of brothers to our other

Life and Work in England

children. When I am a little calmer I shall send you a copy of his last greetings to me. As he wished we shall always think of him as one who has sought and found peace.

With my love, your Mama.

It soon became much worse in Germany. On the 9th November 1938 was the 'Kristallnacht'. In all the large cities of Germany there was a terrible outbreak of hooliganism against the Jews. Houses were broken into, robbed, precious works of art and furniture were thrown into the streets and the windows of Jewish shops were smashed.

My aged mother, sister and brother-in-law still lived in complete seclusion and peace in Bad Homburg, cared for by a faithful old servant. My sister-in-law Gustel remained true to them and often visited them with the little Carla although the journey from Zittau in Saxony to Bad Homburg was a rather lengthy affair. Also some old friends regularly visited my relations in Bad Homburg, including my dear old Professor Martin Möbius and his good wife, who had in fact left Frankfurt and retired to Bad Homburg. Also Dr Georg Eberlein and Nora, his wife, were regular visitors to my sister and brother-in-law. Dr Eberlein had been Mayor of Bad Homburg, but had been dismissed under the Nazis because of his liberal political outlook, but after the defeat of the Nazis returned to an honourable post as a 'Landrat'. My brother-in-law, aged 75 in 1938, had heart trouble, which finally caused him to take to his bed in 1939. So my sister had to look after both her 90-year-old mother and her invalid husband. Brother-in-law Julius died in June, 1939, from his heart complaint. Now I would gladly have brought my unprotected mother and sister to England. But I already had five nieces and nephews here, who came to England through me, as well as my brother Otto's wife, and I was already trying hard to bring Otto over. To achieve this I had to overcome great difficulties, for England no longer allowed emigrants in without justification. Although Otto had the prospect of a post as a professor of psychiatry in Sucré in Bolivia, and only wanted to stay temporarily in England, an English citizen had to vouch for him. Just a week before the outbreak of war, before the door closed so to speak, we finally succeeded in bringing him here. Even with superhuman efforts I could then not have succeeded in bringing my mother and sister over. The first Mrs Bertrand Russell, whom I met in Crosby Hall, vouched for my brother. She invited my brother and me to tea once, otherwise she had not to do anything. Nevertheless, whoever gives a guarantee must always be aware that he or she may become positively involved; so I was grateful to her. In fact my brother should have travelled to South America by the ship *Reina del Pacifico* after a short stay in England. But war broke out and the ship was used for purposes other than passenger transport. Because of this he had to stay a few weeks in England until a passage could be found for him on another ship. After a short visit to his wife and children in Bournemouth he returned to me and we lived together for a few weeks in my little flat in Chelsea, to which I had moved after my three-year stay in Crosby Hall. I made it as comfortable for him as I could and he liked it there. Since we had already had some air raid warnings and I feared we might have some difficulties with the transport arrangements on the morning of his departure we stayed the last night in the Euston Hotel. In the middle of the night the sirens went and we were sent down to the cellar although this, like its predecessors, was a false alarm. The next morning my brother Otto travelled from Euston to Liverpool to embark there. The parting was sad and I never saw him again. He was at first professor of psychiatry at Sucrē, where he was very badly paid. Then he opened a private practice for nervous diseases in La Paz. He was already 60 years old when he emigrated, had to learn a new language and had to work and live in a quite non-European country. His wife and children did not follow him. In his old age he retired to Irupana, a small place on the edge of the virgin forest and there lived as primitively as the indigenous Indo-Spanish population, without any comforts of civilization, but in a good sub-tropical climate at an altitude of about 1000 metres or in the words of my niece in Bogotá: "In the warm country where the coffee grows". My brother and I corresponded regularly and in his last years, with the help of a Canadian friend, I was able to send him a few dollars monthly. He made friends in Irupana with a Dutch Catholic priest and with a German married couple who collected nature objects for a museum. These latter good people cared for him in his last illness and he died, 75 years old, in an American hospital. I shall never forget that my dear niece Carla visited her uncle three months before his death in 1954, from Santiago de Chile to Irupana and so brought him a final great pleasure.

In 1941 there came the greatest worry for my mother and sister in Bad Homburg. They were visited by the police and by the Gestapo. They were to leave their flat, and their servant, the faithful old Anna, was to be taken away from them. We were now in the middle of the Second World War. My dear ones no longer had a moment's peace. My poor sister went out only in the dark of the evening as she did not want to be seen in daylight as a Jewess, wearing the star of David. I remained in contact

Life and Work in England

with them through my friend Helen Schaub in Basle and wished to try to bring them through Switzerland, via Lisbon, and then by aircraft to England. For six weeks I ran from one authority to another in London. I asked my good director, Dr Ledingham, to write to the then Cabinet Minister Sir John Anderson, who was on the Governing Body of the Lister Institute. He did it for my sake, but obviously reluctantly; the decision was negative. I wrote and wired to Basle. My friend wrote and wired to Bad Homburg to my sister and to me in London. In brief: Switzerland said, if England gave an undertaking to accept them there, they would allow them in. England said, when they are in Switzerland they could come to England from there. I had already bought the air tickets from Lisbon to London. My friend in Basle would have received them and paid their fares to Lisbon. I could do no more; I was in real despair. Even my brother in Bolivia could not help. I worked at that time in the branch Institute of the Lister in Elstree, for the Institute in Chelsea had been evacuated because of the bombing. The Director, Sir John Ledingham, also worked and lived there. One evening a telegram came for me from Basle: Dr Ledingham read it and held it back; it was not given to me that evening. The next morning our secretary, Mr Fox, called me into his private flat. His wife gave me a large glass of cognac. Then I was told that my mother and sister were dead. The Foxes did not allow me to go back to the laboratory. About midday (it was a Saturday) my colleague Miss Steabben came and said, "You can't go home to your own flat; you are coming to my home for the weekend". So I spent the weekend with my colleague, her mother and sister, in a little suburban house in Pinner. Next week Dr Ledingham came to me in the laboratory and said, "You must concentrate on your work". I followed his advice, for I still had to take care of my nieces and nephews in England.

In 1941 my sister reacted in the same way as my brother Carl had in 1938. She left a will in which she had arranged to the last detail for the disposition of her possessions. She had also left farewell letters to her nearest. Her moving farewell letter to me I received in its original form only after the war from our friend in Basle. But she sent me at once an English translation since all letters from abroad were also censored here, and so she thought this the right way. I give this letter in full since this document says more than anything I can say.

My dear, faithful Emmy,
    We have been deeply moved and pleased by all the love you have shown us, these recent times from afar. And yet we must now part!

Memoirs

Our dear mother had a good life to the very end, as Gustel and our dear friends here will one day tell you. And all the great troubles of recent years have not been fully realized by her because of her advanced age.

Never, my dear Emmy, have I felt so close to you as in this hour. You have led a brave life and will continue to do so and it is a great comfort to me as I hope that everything will later be well for you and all the dear ones there, to whom I send my heartfelt greetings. For all of you it should be a consolation that I have not to endure dishonour. So many have to lose their loved ones in this war which they did not want; so think of me as a victim of the war and of the times.

With deepest love, with best wishes, content and calm, I embrace and kiss you, your Anna.

My mother was already 93 years old on 4th November, 1941; my sister was 60 years old.

Doctors, out of sympathy, had given my sister and many others the means to end their lives. When one states the number of Jews who were killed by the Nazis, one forgets the great number of those who took their own lives because they knew what lay before them, that is concentration camps and gas chambers.

In spite of the indescribable sorrow which befell my family in the Nazi times yet there are also many good things to record from these years. The reception which we emigrants found in England was extremely generous and sincere, and the human and financial help given to us must make all of us extremely grateful. In May, 1934 I was able to fetch my niece, Liselotte, Carl's daughter, from Dover. The Holiday Fellowship, with which I had long-standing connections, engaged her as a young domestic help. In October she came to me at Crosby Hall and attended the Central School of Arts and Crafts at Southampton Row. She returned to Germany in August, 1935, where she succeeded in obtaining a place training as a hand-weaver. She finally came back to England in January, 1939 and found work as a hand-weaver. My eldest niece, Annemarie, Liselotte's sister, also came over in July, 1939 to train as a nurse. Liselotte has married an Englishman; Annemarie is a nursing sister in a hospital for old patients.

Between the years 1934 and 1937 my brother Otto's three children came to England. First the eldest child, Irmgard, 12 years of age, came and she was educated in a boarding school at Bournemouth (Headmistress: Miss Stocks). Her two brothers Hans and Klaus came to England when they were 14 and 11 respectively and were educated in a boarding school in Durham. All three had scholarships in these schools, although with my small means I helped in little things such as clothing and holidays. Although all this was made possible by my newly acquired friends, yet the help which these schools and their principals were able to give to my nephews and niece cannot be too greatly stressed. All three children also had a university education in England. My niece, Irmgard, married a German teacher after the war, whom she had met here as a prisoner of war, and returned to Germany. My eldest nephew, Hans, is a lecturer in German literature in Dublin. The younger, Klaus, is a civil engineer, married to an English woman and the father of three healthy little boys. They can all thank England for the fact that they now lead decent lives.

Now I return to my own position in the years before the outbreak of the Second World War. At that time I lived at Crosby Hall for almost three years. Here I became friendly with two very fine women. One was Miss Jean Darling. She had studied classics (Classical Tripos) and had finally become a 'housing estate manager' in one of the poorer districts of Chelsea. This was half a social welfare and half a business job, a post under the Town Council. When I moved from Crosby Hall, shortly after she did, we both took small flats in Daver Court, Manor Street, Chelsea. There we saw much of each other. She occupied herself one evening a week with 'Brownies' as a 'Brown Owl' in a poor district of London. Then she would come home late and always had a hot dinner with me. She put a shilling on the table and said "Here is your tip, Emmy" and I tried to give her a good shilling's worth to eat, for then one could buy quite a lot for a shilling! Jean also took me home to her parents, where I once spent a very pleasant Christmas. During the war she was an air raid warden. One night she was with the people of her district in an air raid shelter which received a direct hit. Everyone inside was killed. Jean was one of the most charming and best of women whom I ever had the good fortune to count among my friends. She was very bright, very kind-hearted and with great charm.

I moved during the beginning of the war to a suburb of London near Elstree where I worked. To this place Jean's last letter which follows was addressed.

May 21st, 1940
  Dear Emmy,
    My thoughts are with you and your family just now and I wish that I could give you more practical help than is at present possible. I

know you must be feeling pretty miserable about everything and I am thankful that you at least are naturalized.

It seems a long time that I heard from Frances, but I think that is only because all time passes so slowly just now, and I was all the more impatient for news of her, because it is so nice to get news from a different saner world (America).

Later—I got your letter yesterday and was so glad to hear from you. We must rest assured, that we are thinking of each other just now, even if we don't get time to write. I would simply love to come to you for a weekend, but just at present am not supposed to sleep out of Chelsea. We ought soon to know the worst, I think, and after that I shall know my plans better. I would however love to come over for the day next Sunday, if I can manage it. I now have your phone number so could always let you know any change of plans at the last moment. You will be interested to hear that I have bought a bike, and if it is a fine day I shall cycle over on Sunday.

I feel so anxious about Mummy being on the east coast, and do wish the news could just say whereabouts in East Anglia the bombs have dropped but of course they can't. I am pretty cheerful on the whole, and absolutely confident about the ultimate outcome. I have had a filthy cold which has not made me feel my best. I am so glad to think of you having Liselotte with you just now. She is such a dear, and I did so enjoy seeing her the other day. Hoping to see you next Sunday, June 2nd.

Much love from Jean.

The second friend I made at Crosby Hall was Dr Marjorie Lyon. She was born in Perth, Australia, studied medicine in Sydney and first came to London in 1934 at the age of 29. She specialized in gynaecology and obstetrics and took the appropriate examinations in Edinburgh. In London she worked at various hospitals. At that time we made a number of pleasant Sunday excursions together such as to Kew Gardens, Hampton Court and Windsor. After she left England she entered the Australian Medical Service and served in Malaya where she worked in hospitals in Singapore and Kuala Lumpur. When the Japanese came to Malaya in the Second World War she fled on a ship which was heavily bombed and she found herself suddenly in the water with a number of other refugees. By swimming they reached an uninhabited island where they spent five days without food or water under the tropical sky. Then

Life and Work in England

Japanese soldiers came and took them prisoners. She and her doctor friend Elsie Crowe were taken to a women's prisoner of war camp in Sumatra, where they had to stay until the end of the war. Both worked there under the most difficult conditions in their professional capacities. They were badly treated, neglected and half starved and I'm sure that Marjorie with her unusual courage and capability showed up splendidly in this adversity; she was in fact awarded the O.B.E. after the liberation. Both women were at the end of their resources when the liberating forces arrived. Marjorie was first flown back to Australia, but returned to England for six months in 1947, and we met again. Then just 20 years later, in 1967, she spent her three months leave in England again and our friendship was as firm as ever. Marjorie still works as a schools' doctor in Perth, has a house, a fine garden and a faithful dog. In her large car she has often to travel hundreds of miles with her school nurse and her dog, to visit distant schools. She says, "There is always a room for you in my house". But the journey is a bit too long!

In the years before the war I continued my studies of the PPLO organisms, now called mycoplasmas. With Miss Steabben I worked on bronchiectasis of rats and we studied not only the causative agent but also the clinical and pathological characteristics of the disease. At the second International Meeting for Microbiology held in London in 1936, I spoke on our findings. Dr Øerskov of Copenhagen and Dr Dienes from Boston were also at the meeting and spoke in the same section. In 1938 I published a paper on the differential diagnosis of mycoplasmas from different origins. Afterwards I worked for a time with Dr Findlay and his assistants from the Wellcome Bureau for Scientific Research. In 1933 Dr Findlay had transferred a neurotropic yellow fever virus from mouse to mouse. The infectious material was injected into the brain of the animals. Suddenly Dr Findlay noticed that the infected animals showed nervous symptoms after 48 hours instead of 4 to 5 days which usually happens after injection of yellow fever virus into the brain. Also the symptoms which the mice displayed were different from those produced by yellow fever virus. That is, when the animals were laid on a table they rolled sideways, as a barrel rolls along the ground. Therefore Dr Findlay called this phenomenon 'rolling disease'. Bacteria could not be cultured from the brains of these mice. Nevertheless lesions were found in the brains, in which were present numerous polynuclear leucocytes. Viruses, however, do not cause leucocyte infiltrations. What then was the cause? An unknown organism not readily culturable? It was possible by injection of antiserum against yellow fever to obtain mice which carried only the rolling disease agent. Unfortunately at that point the rolling disease agent was lost by a banal bacterial infection among the mice.

In 1937 something similar occurred in Dr Findlay's laboratory. When the virus of lymphocytic choriomeningitis was passaged through mouse brains the animals died after 2 to 3 days instead of 4 and again exhibited 'rolling'. In the brains infiltrations of polymorphonuclear leucocytes were found as well as very small granules which could be stained by Giesma solution. Dr Findlay believed that the causative agent of the rolling disease in the mice might be a virus; but the polymorphonuclear leucocyte infiltrations spoke against this. When Dr Ledingham heard Dr Findlay's story at a meeting of the Medical Research Club he encouraged him to bring the infected mouse brains to me because Dr Ledingham had an inkling that one of my mycoplasma organisms might be present. I cultivated from the mouse brains a mycoplasma on my special medium. This organism is not found in normal mouse brains but it must be latent in the mice. Dr Findlay had probably exposed it by the injection of the virus. We could not produce the rolling disease by injection of the pure culture of the new mycoplasma into mouse brains. If, however, we injected a sterile nutrient agar suspension together with the culture, the mice developed the typical symptoms. I have generally had the experience that it is difficult or even impossible to produce specific diseases with mycoplasma cultures, unless there is a second non-specific factor present at the same time which enables these organisms to obtain a foothold in the tissue of the animal.

While we were carrying out experiments with our new mycoplasma Dr Sabin in America described 'rolling disease' symptoms in mice whose brains had been infected with toxoplasma. According to his report in the weekly journal *Science* he believed the causative organism to be a virus. I wrote to him and he sent me freeze-dried brains of his mice. From them I obtained cultures which in every respect were identical with ours. I informed Dr Sabin of our results, already described in an article published by the *Lancet*. Dr Sabin now also managed to cultivate mycoplasma from his mouse brains and published his results in an article in *Science* which appeared two weeks before ours. He had neglected to mention us and our correspondence in this article!

I continued to work with Dr Findlay and we now studied a disease of rats which is called polyarthritis. It is, however, not a true arthritis for the joints become oedematous and contain a yellowish pus in which numerous polymorph leucocytes are found. When this joint fluid was streaked on my special nutrient agar a large number of mycoplasma colonies grew up. They could be identified as an organism (L4) which I had previously cultivated from a swollen gland of a rat. If an adjuvant such as, for example, a suspension of agar was added to a broth culture of this L4 organism and the mixture injected intravenously or into the foot of rats severe arthritis could be produced. Thus we demonstrated that the L4 mycoplasma was the causative agent of polyarthritis in rats.

At about the same time Woglom and Warren described a 'pyogenic virus' in rats. Bacteria could not be found in the pus but numerous granules and even thread-like structures were seen. Dr Gye and Dr Knox had injected rats with material obtained from Dr Woglom. The animals which had developed abscesses at the injection sites were handed over to me. I cultivated mycoplasma colonies from the pus and showed that these were identical with the polyarthritis organism; Dr Woglom confirmed my findings. Until the outbreak of the war I studied the different types of mycoplasmas now in my collection and attempted to delimit them from each other by differential diagnostic methods; as the serological method I used agglutination.

Shortly before the Second World War the Third International Congress for Microbiology took place in New York. I had been asked to present a paper and Mrs Neisser hd very kindly invited me to stay with her. I looked forward with pleasure to visiting New York and meeting my foreign colleagues there. But at the last moment I decided not to go, because at that time a war was feared and I still possessed no British passport although I had applied for British citizenship in 1938. Also my brother Otto was here and since his journey to South America was delayed for three weeks by the outbreak of war I was then very glad that I could stay with him in London. People were surprised in New York at my absence and the following item appeared in one of the papers there:

Fate of Woman Scientist Worries Colleagues Here. Delegates attending the Third International Congress for Microbiology at the Hotel Waldorf Astoria expressed grave concern over the fate of one of their colleagues, Dr Emmy Klieneberger, a leader in the field of bacteriology.

Dr Klieneberger was a refugee from Germany, working at the Lister Institute in London. She started for the Congress last week aboard the German Liner Hansa which was ordered to return to Hamburg. It was feared that she had been interned in a concentration camp.

Memoirs

In fact during my last visit to Germany in 1938 I had bought a ticket for the passage in the Hansa, using some of my available German money: but as I explained above I had fortunately called off the journey.

At the beginning of the war the Lister Institute was almost completely closed and working accommodation for the scientists there was found in various other institutes. In the first six weeks of the war a place had still not been found for me. I sat in my small flat in Chelsea and knitted and listened to the radio announcements. To have no work is always a bit depressing; but in those uncertain days it was especially so. However after six weeks I was informed that working accommodation was ready for me in our branch Institute in Elstree. Stables, formerly used for sheep, had been converted into a pleasant laboratory with working benches for two, one for the Director, Dr Ledingham, and one for me. We had gas central heating with a large radiator which made the quarters very comfortable on cold winter days. In winter I wore my old ski-suit and wellingtons because to get to the hot culture room, the refrigerators and the media kitchen I always had to cross fields which were wet and often covered with snow. A technical assistant let me have a room in his house near Watford, about three miles from the Institute, which was in Dagger Lane, Elstree. My host, Clifford Hale, and I cycled to and from the Institute; we had lunch in the Institute and in the mornings and evenings my landlady looked after me. The director rarely came to the laboratory. But he sometimes appeared in the evenings and I then had the opportunity to discuss things with him or show him something, which always pleased me. In an adjacent building Dr Douglas Maclean worked, who was a good colleague of mine, and his young assistant, Dr John Humphrey, who is now a well-known immunologist and F.R.S. I often called him in to show him this or that successful staining reaction under the microscope. Later when I lived with friends in Edgware, he often gave me a lift in his old car and I shall never forget his patient, affectionate and untiring efforts to start the old engine in the cold of winter. Despite all the worries and excitements of the war it was a pleasant and harmonious time in Elstree, on which I look back with pleasure. One became used to the bombing which occurred on and off in the nights and it was a consolation when the only gun in this area drove up and down the Watford Bypass and opened up its anti-aircraft fire. I lived in various places during these years. After half a year with the technical assistant I took a small flat in a working class district in Bushey. I had three rooms with kitchen and bath and a small piece of garden for 19 shillings a week. There I was able to have my niece Liselotte for some time with me, as she, as an 'alien', had to leave the district where she worked. I could also put up once my nephews Hans and Klaus in their six-weeks school holiday.

About that time, Sir John Ledingham proposed I should apply for the D.Sc. of the University of London. I asked him, "Why?" He merely replied, "It would be all to the good". As I now knew my esteemed and respected director very well, I knew two things. The one was that further questions would be in vain. Secondly, he had good reasons for his request and it was always advisable to follow his suggestions. I learned from the Registrar of the University that I could not apply for a D.Sc. degree without already having an English degree, as the former is a higher degree and corresponds approximately to the German Privatdozent qualification. I could, however, on the basis of my German Doctorate receive a Ph.D. degree by retrospectively registering at the London University and sending in a thesis. This was accepted and for the oral examination Sir John and Professor A. A. Miles (now Sir Ashley Miles, Director of the Lister Institute) came to my laboratory and put questions which referred to my special field of work. Afterwards the Ph.D. was granted to me and I immediately sent in my collected publications to the university. Sir Christopher Andrewes was the assessor and in 1942 the university gave me the D.Sc. Shortly afterwards Sir John Ledingham came to me in the laboratory to inform me that I had been made a member of the staff of the Institute. I thought: "So that was the crux of the matter", and I was very pleased about it. In the subsequent war years during which I worked partly at Elstree, and partly, towards the end of the war, again in Chelsea I especially occupied myself with the nuclear structures of bacteria. The reason for this was very simple: in those years I had practically no technical assistance. Also in the department not much special media could be prepared in the media kitchen because of staff shortage. Therefore I restricted myself to culturing bacteria in small quantities and occupying myself with staining methods that revealed the nuclear structures. These investigations I could carry out without technical assistance and problems of morphology had always greatly interested me. In this the discoveries of my friend, Dr C. Robinow (now professor in London, Ontario, Canada) particularly stimulated me. I used extensively the methods he developed and studied anaerobes, actinomycetes and myxococci. The special task I had set myself was to demonstrate the changes in nuclear structures during the development of the cultures. I still remember quite well the astonishment of Sir John Ledingham when I showed him the first nuclear structures of bacteria he had ever seen. We bacteriologists had long believed that bacteria did not possess such structures, since they could not be revealed by the ordinary methods of staining.

At the end of January 1942 Sir John Ledingham retired from his post as Director of the Lister Institute and moved with his family to Mill Hill. When he came to the laboratory for the last time I expressed all I owed to him. He said, "I was very glad to have you; you have been an asset to the Institute". In his taciturn manner, this meant much and I was very pleased about it. Unfortunately he died quite suddenly in May 1944, just 69 years old. I have remained in touch with his family ever since.

In late 1943 I met for the first time the pediatrician from Vienna, Professor Edmund Nobel, through mutual friends. We were immediately mutually attracted and became friends rapidly for we had similar interests and similar tastes. We met regularly twice a week that autumn and winter. On Sundays I visited him and his 90-year-old mother, at his home; and each Wednesday evening we met at the Cosmo Restaurant, which still flourishes at the same place in the Finchley Road. At that time I lived in Edgware and Professor Nobel in Maida Vale. The return home in the blackout with possible air raids and sometimes also thick fog could be difficult but we managed it and it was worth our trouble. Edmund's mother took to me and would have been pleased to see us married. Once she said to me: "You will not regret it, for he is a treasure". Edmund was very devoted to her and his care for her was touching. But she was nevertheless the dominating influence, and I would never have married him while she lived. At the end of the year his mother became very ill with bronchitis and pneumonia and died of this at the age of ninety. Since we were both quite alone we decided to get married. We were married on the 28th January, 1944. We invited my dear friend Mely Hollander and Edmund's friend, Professor Neuburger to an informal lunch at an hotel in Park Lane. Then we spent a long weekend in a pleasant hotel at Brent Bridge near Edgware. I moved into Edmund's flat in Greville Court, which was fully furnished. The capable housekeeper, from Vienna, Frau Goldbaum, looked after us. Edmund had recently opened a consultant practice at No. 10 Harley Street and more and more patients came. He had an especially endearing manner with children and these were quite accessible to him. Neither of us had been married before, but after a few weeks it was as if we had been happily together in deepest friendship for 20 years. This was not only our own opinion but also that of our friends. We were glad to return home each evening to be together again; I always telephoned him at lunch-time. Unfortunately only months after our

Life and Work in England

marriage Edmund developed a heart complaint. We still believed after his first attack and long weeks in bed that he had recovered and with care could lead a fairly normal life. However the disease progressed. The second year of our marriage was a very difficult one for us both. Yet I was glad and thankful that—with Frau Goldbaum's help—I could console and care for him and that I was able to be with him during his last illness and that he was not alone. He died of an embolism on the 26th January 1946, but before the dreadful final stage of the disease had taken hold; I was with him when it occurred and I am glad to say that the end came so quickly and unexpectedly, that he himself did not realize it. I would gladly talk much more here about my life with Edmund and especially of his life before we met. But Edmund was very reserved and never told me much about his former life. I knew very well that he was a highly respected and capable doctor and also had many friends. He was very musical, had studied music and even passed an examination in it. When I met him he had no piano. Almost the first thing we bought when we were married was an upright piano of good tone; of course, it was no Bösendorfer. But he now played every evening after dinner and I sat next to him and turned the music sheets. Until he left Vienna he had taken lessons with his teacher and friend Professor Erdstein. Edmund went to Pirquet in 1911 and followed him from Breslau to Vienna and this was a milestone in his life. He advanced rapidly in his post at the Kinderklinik and in Pirquet's estimation. He shared with all the other pupils of von Pirquet the honour which they showed this great master; but it was quite in accordance with his nature that he was particularly and deeply devoted to him. It was a terrible blow to him when Pirquet, only 55 years old, and his wife took their lives in 1929. The blow, which the tragic end of this great man was to him was such that he never quite overcame it. He inherited the papers, the diary of Pirquet, the oil painting of his wife Maria, as well as being the executor of the will. Yet Edmund never discussed with me or anyone else the reasons for Pirquet's act, he had even destroyed the diary. He obviously did not want any false light to be thrown on the great man. So he buried everything in silence. Also I never asked Edmund to discuss these matters with me. I knew he had reasons for his silence. What Edmund himself represented, what he had done for children, whom he loved, is best seen in the obituary which Dame Harriette Chick wrote for the *Lancet* and which I reproduce here:

Memoirs

From the Lancet, *16th March, 1946*

Edmund Nobel, M.D. Vienna

Professor Nobel who died in London at the age of 62, was a distinguished figure in the cause of child welfare. Of Jewish origin, he was born in 1883 in Gran in Hungary. He graduated in 1910 at the university of Vienna and held posts under von Noorden at the first Medical Clinic in Vienna and under von Leube at Würzburg. In 1911 he was appointed assistant to von Pirquet at the Breslau Kinderklinik and shortly afterwards went with von Pirquet to Vienna when Pirquet was appointed Director of the Viennese University Kinderklinik.

Between 1919 and 1922, when the children of Vienna and of all Austria were suffering acutely from shortage of food, Dr Nobel acted as lieutenant to von Pirquet, who was commissioner for the Amerikanische Kinderhilfsaktion. Together they tackled the feeding of Austrian children and Nobel was mainly responsible for organizing daily hot meals for as many as 200 000 in Vienna and the provinces. Once when a disastrous fire destroyed a huge kitchen which served some thousands of children, alternative places were swiftly equipped by his organizing genius and the new distribution centres were working at full strength within twenty-four hours.

In later years Nobel investigated the incidence of goitre among Viennese children and was concerned in measures taken for its prevention by the addition of iodine to one of the sources of the Vienna water supply. This proved so successful that he was asked to visit Belgium and initiate similar measures for the prevention of endemic goitre in that country. He also worked on behalf of the health organization of the League of Nations and was often seen at Geneva as the Austrian representative at international conferences.

When the Nazis invaded Austria in 1938, Nobel was Chief physician at the Mautner-Markhof municipal hospital for children in Vienna. He was removed from these posts on racial grounds and later in the same year denied the right to private practice. It was ironical that the physician, to whom Vienna, and especially the rising generation, owed so much, should have made himself to feel unwanted.

In October 1938, Nobel accepted an invitation from the government of Albania to organize a children's hospital and child-welfare service in Tirana, the capital; but with the Italian invasion in the spring of 1939, he was obliged to relinquish his position. When he arrived in this country as a refugee a few months later he qualified to practise; and he

Life and Work in England

held appointments at Queen Mary's Hospital for children, Carshalton and at the infant clinic of St Pancras Borough Council. He was for several years medical officer to the L.C.C. and to the Essex county council and was finally appointed physician to the Paddington Green Childrens' Hospital. He also established a consulting practice.

A colleague writes:

Professor Nobel had a great reverence for his teacher and old chief, von Pirquet, whom he had succeeded. At Paddington Green he gathered around him a large clientele of mothers, who valued his skill and his gentle manner; it gave him great satisfaction and happiness to be working once again in a childrens' hospital. He was a quiet and kindly physician, who loved the children whom he served.

CHAPTER VII

My Last Working Period until My Retirement

NOW I WAS ALONE AGAIN; I had so wished to pass my later years with a dear companion and to enjoy them with him. I was not yet old at the age of 54. I could probably go on with work for a good many years and perhaps, like my parents, grow old in good health. I felt that an older person needs a companion even more than a younger one; I felt the loss of my dear Edmund very deeply. I was probably rather run down after Edmund's death and in the late summer of 1946 I contracted severe bronchitis and subsequent pneumonia. The prompt advent of penicillin and the rapid decision of the good Dr Loewy to use it roused me from the lethargic state into which I had fallen and in a few days brought me back to consciousness. We still had food rationing at that time, and several friends brought me their only weekly egg and chicken soup, from chicken acquired on the black market, in order to speed up my recovery with the help of Mrs Irma Goldbaum mentioned earlier. I very much enjoyed the juice which she pressed out of tangerines, for oranges and other fruit from the south were not yet obtainable. I recovered slowly but surely and completely. I went back to my work at the Lister Institute.

A good colleague of mine, Professor Walter Morgan, who had many connections in Switzerland, together with a Zürich professor, Professor Grumbach, concocted a plan by which I was to work for a year in the Hygiene Institute at Zürich. It was very difficult and time-consuming, so shortly after the Second World War, to obtain all the necessary papers for a journey abroad and a permission to transfer money. However at last I had assembled everything required and in the spring of 1947 I travelled

Last Working Period

to Zürich together with my good Zeiss-microscope. I crossed from Dover to Calais and from there via Paris to Basle and Zürich. I saw much of the terrible devastation of the war during this journey. The French customs officer looked with suspicion at my microscope and would not believe that I needed it solely for my own scientific work at Zürich, though I showed him a letter from the Secretary of the Lister Institute that confirmed this. I think he did not understand English and so he confiscated my passport. I was not at all worried, but my English co-travellers were and gave me all kinds of good advice. In Paris I contacted a higher official who understood the matter and instructed the custom's officer who then returned my passport to me with fits of laughter.

A room had been taken for me in a very pleasant pension right below the peak of the Zürichberg and I was well looked after there by the good Fräulein König. I could walk to and from the Institute, as this was in fact situated halfway up the Zürichberg in the Gloriastrasse. It was a wonderful spring and summer and every day I could enjoy the wonderful view onto the lake, the beautiful town built on its shores and the hills and mountains. It was so fine and warm that the lake attracted one for bathing and swimming. Once I wanted to swim across the lake; a young assistant from the Institute accompanied me; when we were in the middle he said we had to turn back as we had no boat accompanying us. I followed and thought: half over and back again is as good as a full crossing.

Working in the Institute was pleasant. Professor Grumbach wanted me to study capsule and slime formation in certain bacteria in which he was interested. I succeeded in working out good methods for staining capsules as well as for staining slime. I obtained preparations which photographed well. I discovered that Neufeld's 'capsule swelling' was based on an erroneous conception. Capsules do not swell, but could be made visible by the application of immune serum. With my method I could demonstrate them without immune serum.

I spent my summer holidays at that time in Curaglia on the Lukmanier Pass in a small, completely Swiss, and very reasonable hotel. I made many excursions during these holidays. One day it occurred to me to climb up to the Medelsser Hütte. The signpost said: three hours; but these had been measured by the fox! It was a beautiful day, a gushing stream came down from above. But where was the hut? I had already climbed for a few hours and there I saw it clinging to the rocks, high above. Now I was seized by the mountaineering fever; I *had* to reach the hut! The path led further over a moraine field, but it was well marked.

Then there came still a last stiff ascent. I noticed that someone observed me from above with a telescope. With some trouble I managed it, for I was no longer in practice for climbing. Up there, there was only an old hut warden; he made me a pot of weak tea. I had brought sandwiches with me, but I was not hungry, only thirsty and I drank the tea to the last drop. Then I thought: True, you have climbed up, but how do you get down? I asked the hut warden if he still expected guests. He said: "No one comes up today". I answered: "How can you know this, you have no telephone and no connections to the villages below". He seemed sure to know. I looked already with distrust at the camping mattresses of the hut and found out that the toilet was outside, quite far from the hut. At a height of 2600 m it was surely very cold in the night. Should I, should I not? Yet suddenly there came three men, one old and two younger ones, down from Peak Medels and they said they would descend at three o'clock. So I started—it was just two o'clock—and consoled myself with the thought that at least then the three men would be coming behind me. When with some trouble, I had climbed down for about a quarter of an hour the old gentleman came behind me and said: "I have been watching you; I must help you". He took me by the hand and showed me how to place my feet in the difficult places. He gave me good instruction and told me he was 73 and named Herr Jäger from the Gantrisch Strasse in Bern. I said: "Then in fact I should lead you, not you me". Soon the other men came and we went over the moraines together. Then the men took their leave and I saw them leaping down—they had to catch a bus below—while I climbed down slowly and only got back at nine o'clock. But the men had warned my landlady, so I was expected to be late. A few days later I made the same ascent with another lady from the hotel and her small 10-year-old son and then I managed it easily, but the little boy was exceedingly tired.

    I had yet another strange experience in Curaglia. A Swiss woman suggested that one afternoon we take a simple walk and an old lady and her grandson accompanied us. Then suddenly on our way, the Swiss woman said we had taken a wrong path and the right way lay above us. I volunteered to climb up a steep slope of rock and grass to see if there was a path above. When I had almost reached the top I slid on the wet grass and was just able to guide myself with my legs to a bush. True, I wore mountaineering boots, but I had no stick. I called to those waiting below that there was in fact a path above, but that I could not go any further from where I was without being in danger of falling over the cliffs. They did not hear this latter remark; I saw them turn back and reach the right path.

Last Working Period

From my vantage point I could see a long way; but no one saw me. I was not worried, for the weather was fine and warm and if I did not return to the house in the evening someone would search for me and find me. After about an hour I saw an old peasant woman approaching me. I waved with my handkerchief; she seemed to think it a joke. Then I took off my dress and petticoat and waved with the long white petticoat. This attracted her attention. She came towards me and seemed to grasp the situation. She put a stick into my right hand, grasped me with the other hand and led me to the path above. I gave her five francs and my silk petticoat. She seemed very pleased, although she hardly understood German and spoke only Graubünden Ladin. I sat down on a nearby seat on the path and five minutes later she returned and asked, "Did I really wish to give her the petticoat". I nodded; perhaps she has now given the 'treasure' to her daughter or granddaughter. In the stony Graubünden the people are very poor, men work on road construction and women and old people cultivate the land as far as possible carrying the hay on their backs down to the valley. When my party returned from their walk in the evening they couldn't understand what had happened to me; I told them my story.

On my free Sundays I made many excursions from Zürich; once Fräulein Kaiser, a woman lawyer from Zürich, and I went across the 'Lägern', that is a path in the Jura, along a ridge which gets narrower and narrower. Suddenly we had to cross the rock face in a gulley; this was just possible; then there was a place where the rock path became very narrow and fell away steeply on both sides. Swiss people are used to climbing from childhood; for them such scrambles are nothing, but we were frightened! But helping hands were extended to us and we got across safely. That Sunday the Winterthur Cooperative Association had crossed the Lägern with us. Among them an elderly lady with ordinary shoes and an umbrella! When we arrived in Baden, all of us went to the same popular garden restaurant and refreshed ourselves with coffee and cake.

Actually, I could have stayed a whole year in Zürich. But I heard that many students were expected for the winter term and that my laboratory could not be kept completely free for me. Also it was already very cold in Zürich at the end of October and because of shortage of coal the Institute could not yet be heated. I wrote to the Director of the Lister Institute, then Dr Drury; he replied that my laboratory was available to me at any time. So I travelled back to London on the first of November and found my flat and the Lister comfortably warm. In Switzerland in 1947 I had participated in a meeting of the Swiss Society for Pathology and Bacteriology in Neuenburg, on Lake Neuenburg. I gave a lecture there on the nuclear structures of bacteria and met Professor Tomcsik, the professor at Basle. I saw him and his charming wife in subsequent years a few times in London and in Basle. Strange to say, in the seven months of 1947 I saw very little of the Director of the Institute of Hygiene in Zürich, Professor Hermann Mooser. But the little I saw of him attracted me and I admired his scientific accomplishments and his personality. As I particularly enjoyed holidaying in Switzerland and as I loved the Swiss mountains, in the following years I often travelled through Zürich and I never missed visiting the Institute of Hygiene and Professor Mooser. Our friendship grew; he also did some work in my field and so we became good friends. I am proud to have gained the friendship of this upright, intelligent and warm hearted man and to describe him I would like to quote what Professor Hans Zinsser said about him in his autobiography:

> This lively, kind hearted Swiss was, and is, one of the best scientific observers with whom it has ever been my good luck to co-operate. Without him we should probably have failed. He is a little sturdy bombshell of energy whose brutal honesty has made him many enemies among all but equally honest people. He is now professor at the university of Zürich every inch of his five feet four a man and a scientist; with a mind like a bell and the temperament of a Gatling gun. It was worth the trip to Mexico to know him. The laboratory where we worked together was on a part of the hospital lawn where, in a tent, one of our most brilliant American bacteriologists—Ricketts—died of typhus in 1910.

Professor Mooser worked for 15 years on the diseases caused by Rickettsias, in Mexico, until he was called to the chair of Bacteriology and Hygiene at the University of Zürich. He succeeded in unravelling the etiology of murine typhus which is caused by the *Rickettsia mooseri*. He found that the organism is transferred by the fleas of rats to humans. Our friendship continued in our retirement and we exchanged letters. I should like to quote some of his which gave me great pleasure:

> As always, your letter gave me great pleasure because it told me that you are well. I was almost two months in Mexico, from whence I returned in mid-June. I have my son from my first wife there. I am pleased that you are considering treating the PPLO in Kikuth and Grumbach's textbook. No one can do it as well as you. . . Here it

Last Working Period

has been extremely hot for the past week, which I can not only bear but even enjoy. Just now, as I write to you—10 a.m.—the thermometer in my room, which only gets the sun in the afternoon, reads 26 °C.

Because there is no place open to me in my former institute I pass the time practising my Latin. I have already read Caesar's *Bellum gallicum* or *Commentarii de bello Gallico*. I took up the grammar beforehand, practised hundreds or learned again many hundreds of verbs and other vocabulary. Afterwards it went amazingly easily. Only occasionally a German text helped me along in some long complicated passage. I shall now take up *De bello civili*. Naturally, I am anxious about your new book. I admire your joy in creation and your literary fecundity. Thank you very much for your last letter. I am greatly pleased every time I see and recognize on the envelope your fine, clear and vigorous writing. This time I am especially pleased with the news of the long flowering of your Saint Paulia. Ours also is in full bloom from June until the first week in December. . . My condition has not improved. It is a pity, I so like eating good things, which now 'digest' badly. . .

5.4.1965

Your visit would, of course, give me much pleasure, at any time except 11th–13th May since I shall be in Basle then, if I am well enough to manage it. I have read the paperback*. How small and unimportant one appears when one comes merely indirectly through a book, in contact with real genius. In addition to Einstein, I admire especially Bethe and, of course, also Pauli, whom I knew personally. After the speeches of appreciation, which were delivered, among others, by Niels Bohr and by Weisskopf—both are mentioned in the book—Rutziska (Nobel prize: Chemistry) said to me "Instead of Pauli one of us should have died; I should gladly let you go first." At the moment it looks as if his wish is going to be granted. (At the moment I'm allright).

With all good wishes, Your friend, H.M.

3.8.1965

Could you please keep the 13th free for me, as long as this fits in with your plans. In any case you must have lunch or rather the mid-day meal with us. I hope very much the weather will improve which has not been the case for some time here. On the 16th August we are going to Locarno, to the Hotel Reber, for a week. It is terribly expensive but

---

* *Brighter than one thousand suns*, by Robert Jungk.

is the only hotel with its own bathing beach. My wife loves swimming and I gladly spend money on her. Since I have retired we no longer have a cook, not even a help, because we can no longer afford this so that my wife has thoroughly earned expensive holidays. Have you any special wishes for the menue for the 13th? Don't be modest, because for what gives you the most pleasure is just what is good enough.

6.11.1966

It is such a pleasure to have your friendship. I was greatly touched by your telephone call... I am quite well, at least I have no pains to speak of. I read almost all day, in the morning usually in bed. I was very pleased recently about the award of the Nobel Prize to Dr Peyton Rons and for the letter he wrote to me. "Our friendship has been one of the greatest joys of my life." I didn't know he thought so much of me. I must tell you what I read: three times a day, of course, *Die Neue Züricher Zeitung*. It may interest you to know that a Miss Rothschild—of the famous family—a few years ago wrote the history of the N.Z.Z. Then I read Roman authors in Latin. I started with Caesar's *Commentarius de bello Gallico*, books about the civil war, the Alexandrian, African and Spanish wars. I have *Time* every week. Unfortunately I have no dictionary to look up the many American words. An Englishman said, "It's true, we have much in common with the Americans except language." But I like the Americans, or America.

Greetings from your friend, H.M.

21.12.1966

I am deeply moved by your goodness and friendship. Your letter came today and as my depression is rather less I was able especially to enjoy it. Alan Moorehead's blue and white Nile I have. I have even read these books twice. You have no reason to be modest about going into print yourself. You have a *good* reputation and have the gift of expressing your results in a masterly way. Now I am anxious about your new "little book", as you call it, and I am pleased about the heralded "paperback". I read more English publications than German. Biographies, travel and history interest me most. At present I am sorry for Chancellor Erhard. I am no friend of the Germans but I am sorry that now the Arabs go on about them. This doesn't require much courage.

Last Working Period

28.12.1966

Your telephone call pleased me very much. You have become a true friend to me. That this should come to me in my old age is wonderful. I have another true friend in New York, that is Peyton Rous... I am quite allright—now and then physically and mentally a little up and down. I was never a 'happy' person, generally too inhibited to be really free and quite happy. Yet now I think daily of my mother, who sacrificed herself for her husband and the numerous children and who died much too early. I hope very much that you can fully enjoy your life even if it is difficult for me to imagine this in view of the inconceivable sorrow that has descended on the Jews of Germany and other lands. I, myself, who have no Jewish blood cannot escape from it. I have just been reading *Lords of the Atlas* by Gavin Maxwell. It is an account of the recent history of Morocco. These lords, the heroes of the book were a hateful mixture of gentlemen and filthy swine. A comparison with the politicians of the 'great nation' at that time however is by no means to their (the lords) disadvantage...

4.4.1967

You are lucky with your flowers. Our St Paulia does not bloom, and what saddens me still more is that only one of the two Amaryllis flowers. The two stems, after the winter rest produced immediately strong tall leaves, over one metre. Also the two stems of Sprekelia formosissima produce this year excessive leaf growth. I had brought the bulbs from Mexico. It is a lily of light red colour and of quite unique shape; that is, the blooms. I am much the same, sometimes rather better then soon rather worse. I slowly accustom myself to ill health. On May 3rd I shall be 76. That is quite something!

5.12.1967

Now you are preparing for the second journey to distant Colombia. I wish you a fine, trouble free journey and everything of the best in the sunny highlands of Colombia. Thank you for the detailed account of your return route. I was never in Colombia—know the country only from books, journals, newspapers. The last thing I read about the country is the book by Salvador de Madariaga, *Biography of Bolivar*. Recently I have been much better. Since intensive therapy with antibiotics the fever bouts have disappeared and the urine is at last sterile. I hope it will remain so. I have forgotten the botanical name of the Euphorbiacea which we call Christmas Star, named Noche buona in Latin America. Three years ago I succeeded in the artificial fructification of our amaryllis. Numerous offspring came from the seeds—so numerous I didn't know what to do with them. Unfortunately it is 3 to 4 years before they bloom. Perhaps it will be this year or next year.

22.9.1970
Dear Doctor Nobel,

I write "Dear Doctor" not as the conventional form for a letter, but because to me and undoubtedly to many others you are a fine and dear human being. This is also proved to me by your admiration for Laurens van der Post. Many thanks for the book *The night of the new moon*. I read it immediately, then I asked my wife—I was in bed—to bring me from my small library *The lost world of the Kalahari* and I read it for a second time. If all people were like van der Post the world would be different—I mean humanity. I fear for Israel. It would be terrible if the Jews had to flee again in a diaspora. Einstein once said about the almost complete destruction of the eastern Jews, "How much genius has been lost in this way." I found this statement heartless. I thought of the terror and the sorrow thrust upon these people. Even the majority of non-geniuses (genii) can suffer.

I am not well, my main complaint is incurable, but my mind is still intact. I can still read and think about what I read.

Many thanks for your true friendship, Your H.M.

Dear friend,

I shall send you a few lines before you depart for distant Australia. Firstly I have to thank you for your welcome letter. I admire your fine handwriting with each letter. It is so clear and legible, like the writer herself. When one writes a letter the purpose is to give no difficulty to the recipient in understanding what one wants to say. Unfortunately many people do not do this. Today I write slightly crookedly, because I am writing in bed. I wish you the best possible journey. I shall be 80 on the 3rd May. It will probably be my last birthday. I am confined to bed; I read much. At the moment Antonia Fraser's *Mary, Queen of Scots*. Queen Elizabeth of England doesn't 'come off' very well.

Greetings and all good wishes for the journey.

Last Working Period

When I came back from my Australian journey the dear professor was no longer with us. He had suffered a lot before the end.

As can perhaps be seen from the preceding letters, he was a very versatile personality with a wide variety of interests. Apart from science and medicine they included mathematics, languages (he was a great linguist), history and politics. His general knowledge was amazing. As a bacteriologist he had great imagination, great power of observation and boundless enthusiasm. However his humaneness, his sympathy with the oppressed and helpless and his hate for all that was evil, wicked and unjust were some of his most outstanding traits of character. His intelligence, his judgement, his scientific achievements were widely acknowledged and confirmed by three honorary doctorates. His uncompromising honesty was not liked by everybody and if Hitler had conquered Switzerland he would have been one of the first to find himself in a concentration camp. Yet his great and original personality, his integrity and most of all his warm heart could only be fully appreciated by those who had the good luck to win his friendship.

Some time after the war, when conditions had become normal, I started to work again in my own special field on the L-phases of bacteria and on mycoplasmas. I then showed that the L-phase of *Streptobacillus moniliformis* could be filtered through gradocol membranes which will not pass bacteria, and also that the filterable elements are approximately the same size as the elementary particles of the biggest viruses. In the year 1957 I published a historical review of the so-called 'filterable forms of bacteria' and thus entered upon uncertain and shaky ground, for the filterability of bacteria was a much disputed subject. The scientists who supported this theory explained it by the bacteria possessing a virus phase. Many of the older, well-known and esteemed scientists such as Almquist, Friedberger (*kryptogenes Virus*), Hadley, Mellon, Levaditi, Loehnis, Nicolle, etc. believed that the mysterious, hidden, virus form could regenerate bacteria, which would then thrive anew to bring about a fresh outbreak of the infectious diseases. However I was not convinced by this theory but I found the study of early research very interesting and suspected that the filterable L-phase of the bacteria could be adduced to explain some of the positive filtration results of the early scientists. This article brought me a very interesting and enjoyable correspondence with Dr Mellon and Dr Hadley and also two invitations to Lausanne from Professor Hauduroy.

Also at this time the London University gave me a grant to procure a phase microscope. This wonderful instrument, for which I had had an incubator made, gave the greatest pleasure to me and my technical assistant; with it we could make continuous observations, at 37 °C, on growing cultures and photograph the changes we saw, every 20 minutes; sometimes in our enthusiasm, we ate no lunch in order not to interrupt our observations and miss something.

One of my first invitations abroad after the war came in 1948 from Professor Boivin. A congress was being held to celebrate the centenary of the Société de Biologie, in Paris. Boivin who held the chair of bacteriology in Strasbourg, was also interested in the nuclear structures of bacteria and he and his pupils Tulasne and Vendrely had published papers about this. Professor Tulasne was unable to attend the congress, but both Boivin and Vendrely were present. My lecture was well received in Paris and I had stimulating discussions with both men. Professor Boivin invited Dr Vendrely and me for lunch in a well-known comfortable Paris restaurant 'L'Alsacienne' and we. had 'truit' and drank Sauterne with it. When I remarked that wine was not necessary, the professor replied, "But my name is Boivin". I was very sorry that only a few years after this gay and stimulating meeting, Professor Boivin, at the age of 54, died of a disease of the spinal cord. His successor in the chair at Strasbourg was Professor Tulasne whom I frequently met at congresses in the following years. He was particularly interested in the L-phases of bacteria.

In 1949 I was again in Switzerland for some weeks. On the way I stopped in Amsterdam, where I stayed with Dr Wout van Iterson, the well-known electron microscopist, and I also met Professor Charlotte Ruys for the first time. In Amsterdam, Zürich, and on my return journey, in Munich, I gave lectures. Professor H. Braun, who now had Pettenkofer's chair in Munich, persuaded me to stay for a few days in Munich. We had not seen each other since 1933 when we had both left the Institute of Hygiene in Frankfurt, he for Istanbul, I for London. Although he had not always been very friendly to me in Frankfurt, now he was extremely amiable.

In spring 1953 Professor Hauduroy invited me to Lausanne, where I met mostly virologists, including Professor Kenneth Smith (Cambridge), Dr Lépine (Institut Pasteur, Paris) and Professor Penso (Rome). I also met there Professor Zavagli from Rome, the agalactia specialist, who subsequently proved a very valuable adviser and a source of material of agalactia in sheep. This congress in Lausanne was an intimate meeting and gave an opportunity for personal discussions between colleagues. Our papers were published in a little volume under the title *Problèmes actuels de Virologie* by Masson & Cie, Paris, with a foreword by Professor Hauduroy. He believed he had a method which could demonstrate that bacteria had a virus form. His pupils shared his belief. I learned this method in Lausanne; it consisted of filtering cultures through a filter which retained bacteria, then streaking the filtrates on plates, flooding these plates with broth and renewed streaking, etc. I carried out tests in London in accordance with Hauduroy's instructions and found that one always obtained bacteria, after a number of manipulations, since even with the most careful work contamination cannot be avoided. I stored clear filtrates up to two years and found that after such a long time something had grown in each ampoule. I could not be converted to the views of the worthy and amiable Professor Hauduroy. There seem to be always air contaminations which develop reluctantly and late.

At the end of my stay in Lausanne I spent a holiday in Glion, above the lake of Geneva. I had hoped for an invitation to the Sixth International Congress for Microbiology in Rome, in September; but Professor Stuart Mudd, who led the section on morphology of bacterial cells, was not well disposed towards me as we had had a slight controversy over one of his published electron micrograms. Then suddenly, in Glion, I received a telegram from Professor Piekarski, from Bonn, saying that I should go to Rome to talk on the L-phases of bacteria. The Lister Institute gave £50 for the journey, so I gladly accepted the invitation. The Rome Congress, in fine September weather, was one of the best I have ever attended. I arrived five days before the congress and stayed on a few days in order to see something of Rome. The outward journey with Dr Anne Mayr-Harting and her 16-year-old son Henry, who was interested in everything, had a note of gaiety and we enjoyed ourselves even when we had to wait at the airport four hours for the departure of our flight. In Rome there were several receptions for the members of the congress. One evening we were invited by the municipal authorities to the Capitol, where we were 'wined and dined' generously on a large terrace where an orchestra played. In the centre was a large table with cold meat dishes, salads, fruit and drinks etc., all beautifully arranged. But the congress members were not dignified; or had outsiders gatecrashed? People fell upon the table like rats and crowded around it. I did not want to push forward and was willing to forego all delicacies. I stood alone, apart; then a Dr Cajus, a delegate from Malta, introduced himself to me. I said, "I come from the Lister Institute in London". He asked, "Klieneberger?" I confirmed this; then my 'Maltese Knight', as I called him, found me a table and a chair and brought me a wonderful plate of meat, salads and something to drink. He must, indeed, have had a small magic wand. He was a pleasant man and we had good conversation. A similar thing happened on our wonderful excursion to Tivoli. I was with Professor Bob Murray from London, Ontario. Again people thronged around the luncheon buffet. We preferred to sit near the water display and chat. After an hour we returned. Now I found a chair and table where a little later Professor Charlotte Ruys joined me. Then Sir Christopher Andrewes appeared and said, "We have one lunch plate too many, it's for you". Later he sent his daughter with ice cream and fruit for Professor Ruys and me. The meetings were very interesting. Our section was attended by Professor Bob Murray, Professor Anneliese Winkler, Professor Piekarski, Dr Mayr-Harting, Dr Bisset, Dr Vendrely and Dr Delamater among others. Professor Mudd was our chairman. When he became sick I was asked to take over the chair one afternoon. First I thought I couldn't do it; but it went well. In Rome we had many opportunities for discussion, inside and outside the meetings. We only had breakfast in the hotel. Usually at midday we went to one of the small cafés where there were good sandwiches and espresso coffee. In the evenings I was sometimes invited out or there were official receptions like the one on the Capitol. Otherwise I went to one of the rosticcerias; they were the cheapest restaurants in Rome, but the food was quite good there. When I gave my lecture Professor E. G. D. Murray of Montréal was present. Afterwards he talked to me very charmingly and I was always pleased when I met him and his wife again, whose acquaintance I made in London, Ontario. When I returned from Rome at 12 o'clock midnight—at that time I shared a house with my niece Liselotte and her husband Frank—both jumped out of bed, and Smokey, our charming Siamese cat, ran, miaowing loudly, up the stairs to my flat, and all three gave me a hearty warm welcome.

In June 1954, the World Health Organization invited 30 people, some venereologists, some bacteriologists (including myself), to Monte Carlo to exchange views on the problem of non-gonorrhoeal urethritis. I met there old acquaintances such as Professor Tulasne from Strasbourg, Dr Freundt from Copenhagen, Dr Edward from Beckenham (London), Dr Chu from Cambridge and Miss Sarabelle Madoff, Dr Diene's assistant. I met for the first time, Professor Ruiter from Groningen (Holland), Dr Durel from Paris and Dr Harkness, the able and well-known venereologist from London. I was accommodated in a nice hotel, where the 'valet de chambre' opened up a whole suite for me and where I was welcomed with a large bunch of flowers. We had interesting discussions because it is always fruitful when people who from training and profession work in different fields are able to discuss together problems of common interest. Apart from our scientific meetings Monte Carlo had much to offer us. One evening we were driven to Cannes for dinner. One excursion took us to the heights where Monaco's radio transmitter is situated. There were several receptions and on the last evening the 'Gouvernement Princier' gave a dinner in the famous Hotel de Paris where we sat in armchairs at tables which were so wide that we had to shout across them! I always had the 'luck' to have an old gentleman to take me in to dinner, who was either a representative of the government or of the town, with whom I had to converse in French and I was never able to sit with my friends. I went once to the casino, which I found most tedious. I stayed on holiday for another week after the congress and enjoyed the sea and the beautiful beach, which was quite deserted, as the season started much later. I also made excursions into the surrounding country, for example to Mentone, and spent one afternoon in the beautiful Marine Aquarium in Monaco. In Monte Carlo I became friends with Professor Ruiter with whom I corresponded. Funnily enough, we travelled in the same compartment to Monte Carlo but unfortunately discovered that only in the last half hour. On the return journey from Monte Carlo I spent one fine day in Avignon where I found that only half the famous bridge existed, but a guided tour through the palace of the Popes was most interesting. Back in London, Dr Harkness invited me to dinner and we are still friends. As I think very highly of him as a doctor I have in the course of the years sent him many a patient. He treated all of them without charge, out of his kindness and willingness to help.

In 1954 and 1955 I found two very valuable colleagues. I read a paper by Dr Kwok-Kew-Cheng in the *Journal of Pathology and Bacteriology*, in which he described an operation on young rats; this consisted in the tying-off of a bronchus with the result that the animals developed a bronchiectasis. He could not find a causative infection and the 2½-month-old rats which he used seemed, in general, to have healthy lungs. However I knew that these young rats harboured the (L-3) *Mycoplasma pulmonis*, if not in the lungs, then in the nasopharynx and that later they would get the well-known bronchopneumonia. But we had never been able to bring about onset of the disease experimentally. Probably the stagnation produced in the tied-off part of the lung in the

Cheng operation and the lack of aeration gave the mycoplasma an opportunity of multiplying rapidly and causing the well-known lesions. At that time Cheng was working in the Serum Institute at Carshalton, Surrey. He was quite ready to operate on a number of young rats for me. He had tied off lobes of the lungs. After four days the mycoplasma had increased enormously and bronchiectasis was noticeable. After 12 days the disease was rampant and the lungs had already formed abscesses. Thus in an elegant manner proof was given that the etiological cause of rat bronchopneumonia was in fact the *Mycoplasma pulmonis*.

My second collaborator was Mr F.W. Cuckow, who was then working in the Chester-Beatty Institute for Cancer Research. There they had a fine electron microscope and Mr Cuckow, who was a physicist, could use it with the skill of an expert. For a long time I had wished to investigate mycoplasmas under the electron microscope and now at last I had the desired opportunity. We needed quite a time until we had found the right method of preparation for my delicate organisms. Then finally we were successful and obtained satisfactory electron micrographs, which pleased me greatly and agreed well with the earlier photomicrographs.

In May 1956 I was again invited to Lausanne by Professor Hauduroy to a 'Study Session' on "Les Formes L et les Formes Évolutives des Bactéries". There I met old friends again, including Professor Tulasne. Up to the end of his life Professor Hauduroy believed in the filterable bacterial virus, which in 1924 he described as invisible, in a book which at that time aroused much attention. But with him this belief has died. Will this mystic idea return once again? In my youth many scientists believed that different bacteria which were actually well differentiated could change into each other. In this connection Professor Henneberg, the editor of the *Zentralblatt für Bakteriologie*, wrote to me as follows, "I believe in science it is 20 to 30 years before old ideas are brought back freshened up as new ones. I am continually getting papers for the *Zentralblatt* on conversion-forms and such things: a fraction reaches publication, because there must be an outlet for things which are neither sinful nor dangerous which we accept from authors and offer our readers".

Among the colleagues whom one meets during one's lifetime there are always some outstanding by their scientific achievements together with their human qualities. If people such as these, well-known internationally by all the people working in the same field, possess integrity, humanity, modesty and personal charm one cannot but be greatly attracted by them. Such a man, who also emigrated from Germany to England under the Nazis, was Professor Carl Prausnitz-Giles. He was of half English and half German-Jewish extraction and had English as well as German medical qualifications. He had spent part of his youth and his early working life in England. Later he was appointed to the chair for Bacteriology and Hygiene at Breslau University as successor to the famous Professor Pfeiffer. Prausnitz was one of the most esteemed German professors. His work on allergy and hay-fever was known world-wide. I met him first in 1936 at the occasion of the International Congress for Bacteriology and Hygiene in London. Shortly before this he had opened a medical practice at Ventnor (Isle of Wight) together with an English boyhood friend. He soon became greatly appreciated by his patients as a first class doctor. He also established a private laboratory at his home 'Kingseat'. I was very pleased when I met him a second time in 1959 when he had been called upon to deliver the 'Jenner Memorial Lecture' at St George's Hospital in London. I have kept his charming letters received subsequently. Here they are:

Kingseat, St Boniface Rd, Ventnor, Isle of Wight, 16th June 1959
My dear Frau Klieneberger-Nobel!

Thank you very much for your kind letter. I am writing only today because first I wished to read your papers. The kind words which you wrote about my paper touched me. But I had, and was aware of it, nothing new to offer. I had hoped to give the younger generation a short review of the development of the allergy and to indicate some unresolved problems. I cannot tell the Old Guard anything new! I am all the more grateful for your words.

I have read of your fine work with great interest. What work you have put into this interesting problem, which you first discovered! How many new and interesting results you and your other research workers have obtained! My thoughts revert to the time when pathological bacteria were discovered and their relative uniformity and immutability believed in. Then came something strange. Theobald Smith discovered an invisible cause of disease, the virus of swine fever. And today viruses are almost as familiar to us as the bacteria.

But the L-forms are yet somewhat stranger. When something quite different can arise from a bacterium, a cell-wall-less microbe with ill-defined surface limits and from this are produced still much smaller similar life forms, which again grow into the large form and that under certain conditions the original bacteria can arise again from this culture form. This is an almost incomprehensible thing! It no longer fits into the old concepts.

Memoirs

I am surprised how little has been done serologically in the matter. I should like to think that here is a wide-open field for research.

I should especially like to say how I am filled with admiration for your wonderful techniques. Thank you very much for the papers, both on the L-forms and the PPLO, from which I have learned much.

Every good wish and success for your further work, Carl Prausnitz

1960
Dear Frau Klieneberger-Nobel!

It was a great pleasure to see you again before the year was over. Since then I have in a sense met up with you again, for I have read your book on PPLO. I should like to wish you all success with the book. It gives such a clear and at the same time critical account of the results of the work of yourself and of other research workers. I have learned much from it and wish to thank you for this.

Best wishes, Carl Prausnitz

3rd October 1961
Dear Dr. Klieneberger-Nobel!

It was very kind of you to send me the reprint of your paper on the PPLO organisms. I have read it with great interest and learned much from it, both on the theoretical and the practical sides. You have led us very far into this interesting borderland between bacteria and viruses and I hope your further researches will succeed in building up still further the systematology of these fascinating microbes. The practical importance in the pathology of various hitherto imperfectly understood syndromes is indeed most interesting and may have far-reaching consequences. I hope we may meet and have a talk about your work some day.

Meanwhile I remain with very kind regards, Yours sincerely, C.P.G.

In 1958, in February, I attended the meeting of the Austrian Society for Microbiology and Hygiene, which was held amid deep snow and beautiful sunshine on the Semmering. Here again I met Professor Bieling, who had invited me. He became a lecturer under Professor Neisser at the Frankfurt Institute of Hygiene; I had not seen him since 1933, that is for 25 years. He was now acting professor of Bacteriology and Hygiene in Vienna. I also met Professor Henneberg, the director of the Robert Koch Institute, there; and also Professor Hugo Braun, Professor Anneliese Winkler and Professor Piekarski were there. I gave a

Last Working Period

paper on L-phases and there was a lively discussion on it afterwards. The German colleagues gave me a friendly welcome. It is a great mistake to assume that the majority of the academic classes sympathized with the Nazis. But what could they do under the thumb of criminals! Therefore I was very pleased when on my 75th birthday I was made an honorary member of the Robert Koch Institute and shortly afterwards was named as corresponding member of the German Society for Bacteriology and Hygiene. Also the charming and truly sincere letters I received on that occasion from German colleagues pleased me.

Here I want to add that I do not feel any resentment towards the Germans as a people. If the German people—*as a whole*—are guilty for the appalling crimes of the Nazis then I and all those Jews who—as well as their ancestors—who lived up to that time in Germany as German citizens share the guilt with them.

In the fifties I was requested by the Medical Research Council Working Party to work with them on the problem of non-specific urethritis. It was interesting for me to find to what extent *Mycoplasma hominis* played a part in the manifestations of this disease. St Mary's Hospital (Dr Csonka) and the London Hospital (Dr Oates, Dr Caterall) supplied us with material. Firstly we tried to produce cultures from the discharges from the patients and to determine how many cases gave positive results. A collaboration between laboratory workers and clinicians is in the first place a problem of human relationship. The suitable choice of cases for bacteriological investigation, the accurate knowledge of the case history, the sampling of material, the rapid transfer of the material from patient to the nutrient medium of the bacteriologist are factors of prime importance to the success of such studies. The clinicians want to cure their patients, the bacteriologists want to solve a scientific problem. It was soon clear to me that practical collaboration was only possible when we spent much time in the clinics, visiting the doctors there and being present when material was taken, streaking it directly onto plates brought with us and making notes of that part of the case history in which we were interested. It was also important to follow the subsequent course of the illness and its cure. The study of our problem was made difficult in that the patients who come to venereological polyclinics are often unreliable and do not attend regularly or stay away completely. In the early days of this investigation when we were mainly concerned with culturing of mycoplasma, I was faithfully assisted by the capable Dr Bill Blyth, who gained his Ph.D. at the Lister Institute and is still on the staff there. After that until my retirement a scientific assistant was engaged to work with me. Her main task was to investigate, in accordance with a programme devised by me, human sera for antibodies against *Mycoplasma hominis*. The studies on cultures had convinced us that this mycoplasma is responsible for a certain kind of non-specific urethritis. So I hoped for much from these serological investigations and I was not disappointed. My first assistant stayed only a short while with me; she had to return to Australia because her mother fell ill. Dr Dorothy Card (Perret) was my next capable and amiable assistant. We worked together successfully for some years. She left me when she married Dr John Perret and returned to her home with him in Western Australia. She now works there in Perth for the Public Health Authorities. I then succeeded in securing Dr Ruth Lemcke, whom I had already known for some years, as my collaborator. She stayed with me until I retired in 1962. We became good friends and she made a name for herself throughout the world in her field of work; she is now a member of the staff of the Lister Institute and well known as a specialist on mycoplasmas. I would like to mention that during my last years at the Lister Institute Dr Ruth Wittler, who had formerly worked with me, came for half a year to work with me again. We have also remained good friends. In autumn 1958 I moved from Sidcup in Kent back to London and since then I have lived in a handsome sunny flat in north-west Hampstead. Commuting to and from Kent to the Lister Institute by train or in my own car became too strenuous over the years and I was also too far away from my old friends; because in old age one needs friends of one's own generation, although it is wonderful to have contacts with the younger generation. From my present flat I was able to drive through Hyde Park to the Lister Institute in 25 minutes.

Shortly after my move at the end of 1958, I travelled to New York for our first Congress on Mycoplasmas. I travelled on the *Media*, a freighter of the Cunard Line, taking eight days from Liverpool to New York. This ship can take 150 passengers; but as it was mid-winter there were only 25. We had the best cabins; in any case, there was only one class on the ship. It was a wonderful crossing. In the evenings we gathered together for bingo, charades and 'horse-racing'. The ship's purser saw to our good entertainment. We went to bed between 12 and 1 o'clock in the morning I did not come up on deck much before 11 o'clock. To realize what an enormous extent of water the Atlantic Ocean is, one must at one time have crossed by ship. When we arrived in New York, the Hudson was frozen over and the picture it presented made me think of Antarctica. It was wonderful when we first saw the Statue of Liberty and the skyline of

Last Working Period

Manhattan. As soon as the ship docked a telephone was installed and I could announce my arrival by telephone to Dr Ruth Wittler. At her request I went to Washington D.C. for two days and we travelled together to the Congress, which was held in the Barbizon Plaza Hotel and which was very well attended. The sessions were interesting in parts but not well organized and speakers who had not much to say were allowed unlimited time to say it. I met there my old friend, Dr Louis Dienes, whom I had not seen since 1936. In the meantime we had had many controversies in print which did not affect our friendship. He invited me for a week to his house in Cambridge, Massachusetts (Boston), where he lives with his children, the Tafts. Both the Tafts are pathologists and work in the Massachusetts General Hospital where Dr Dienes also has his laboratory. I gave two papers in Boston, one of them at Harvard University. Otherwise I spent the days with Dr Dienes as he wished and was used to. At ten o'clock we drove to the hospital and spent the day with Miss Sarabelle Madoff in the laboratory where Dr Dienes showed me a great deal and where there was much to discuss. One day we made an excursion to the wonderful coast of Massachusetts, to Nahant, and the old port of Salem. The coast has rocky inlets and reminds one very much of the English coast of Cornwall, across the Atlantic Ocean. Altogether I was six weeks in North America. Besides Boston and New York, I visited Chicago, where I also lectured and stayed with my old friend, Liesel Schmitt. One of the most beautiful days of the whole journey was the one I spent at 'Great Lakes', one and a half hour's drive from Chicago. There was a 'Naval Unit' of bacteriologists; Lieutenant Gutekunst, a tall, well-built, pleasant young man, drove me there and back! Captain Miller was the Head of this unit's laboratories. We found much to discuss after my lecture and I also very much enjoyed the drive along the enormously extensive Lake Michigan. From Chicago I was called back to Washington by the National Institute of Health in Bethesda, where I gave two lectures. Finally I went by the Canadian Pacific Railway to London, Ontario, Canada. In the train I took a 'roomette', where one has an easy chair, a wall-bed and washing facilities all to oneself. The whole night I lay on my bed looking through the window on to the expanses of snow, gleaming in the moonlight, broken here and there by a few buildings, surrounded by trees, and I dreamed of the immense rippling golden yellow fields of wheat, which covered these wide plains in summer. In St Thomas, where I had to get out, Dr Robinow and his son Tony fetched me at 5 o'clock in the morning in the depth of winter and in the icy cold, to drive me by car to their home in

London. I stayed there one week, gave a lecture and renewed my acquaintance with Professor Bob Murray and his father Professor E.G.D. Murray and his dear wife Freda.

I must add that of all the large cities of North America which I saw on this journey, I particularly liked Boston and Washington with their wide avenues. In all these towns one finds the most beautiful museums and to study European painting one can confidently go to Washington, Boston or Chicago (not to speak of New York) where there is an astonishing wealth of famous painting.

In May 1962, I had suddenly to undergo an operation for gall-stones. In spite of this, because I made a good recovery, I was able to attend the International Congress for Microbiology, in Montreal, on August 8th. There 13 different symposia were running at the same time; one of them was dedicated to Mycoplasmas. Professor Harry Morton of Philadelphia was our chairman and I had to give the first lecture. So many people came that at the start of my lecture, the hall had to be enlarged, for which there were good facilities in the Queen Elizabeth Hotel. Dr Louis Dienes spoke after me; I was with him a great deal during this Congress. We went together on the beautiful excursion into the mountainous surroundings of Montreal. Dienes especially liked to talk far into the night. Since he used to withdraw from six to nine to sleep he was still fresh into the middle of the night, but I, having different sleeping habits, was not so good at this. Professor E.G.D. Murray was President of the Congress. He had an upstairs suite in the Queen Elizabeth Hotel and invited guests there after dinner. Once I was invited with the Robinows to him and his dear wife and spent a very pleasant hour there. I think that was the last time that I saw this highly respected and very much loved professor.

The Congress dinner in the Queen Elizabeth Hotel was very grand and attended by thousands of people. I sat at a table near the podium and so could hear all the speakers very well, but the wittiest and the best speech was, of course, made by my 'Chief', the Director of the Lister Institute, Sir Ashley Miles, because he is, without doubt, the best after-dinner speaker I have ever heard. At the table beside me sat Professor Ouchtolony with whom I had good conversation. Not only had he discovered the method bearing his name but had also travelled for two months throughout North America with his numerous children and wife, camping in the open.

Shortly after this congress, on October 1st 1962, I retired from my work at the Lister Institute. I was over 70 years old and although still quite healthy I thought and still think that at a certain age one should

Last Working Period

give up scientific work and hand over to younger people even if one has still the capacity to go on working. Advances are so rapid in our field of work today that in old age one cannot keep up with them and it is right to 'close the account' and occupy oneself with other things. I now have more time to look after my old friends, who need me, as I need them. I sometimes have guests to lunch or dinner. In my bay window and on my balcony I even have a small garden and instead of bacteria I rear African violets, geraniums and fuchsias. And I have even found time to write a second book, in addition to my first on the mycoplasmas, which appeared in 1962. This second one was of a semi-popular nature about bacteria and was published in 1965; it is called *Focus on Bacteria*. I was helped with extreme kindness by Sir Graham Wilson in its compilation and correction. He came to me several times, on his bicycle (with which—although no longer young—he crosses London!) in order to discuss details with me or even to bring along books for me because he found they were too heavy for me.

As I have visited my niece Carla in Bogotá (Colombia) twice in recent years I was stimulated to learn Spanish and I propose continuing with this as it is a beautiful language and there is so much interesting literature.

On the second of October 1962, when I retired from work, my colleagues at the Lister Institute gave me a farewell dinner in St Stephen's Restaurant, opposite the Houses of Parliament. Seventeen colleagues came and this occasion gave me immense pleasure. The Director, Sir Ashley Miles, took me to the table and gave a speech in which—this I found especially charming—he spoke not of my scientific capabilities but only of my personal qualities. And indeed he picked out three characteristics; my courage, my honesty and—to my astonishment—my charm. That was pleasant for an old woman to hear!

Although I no longer worked as a bacteriologist I was, astonishingly, invited in 1965 to the second congress on the Biology of Mycoplasmas, in New York, by the New York Academy of Sciences. The meetings were held in the Waldorf-Astoria Hotel, and, compared with our first meeting seven years earlier, it was a very large assembly. It was very interesting to hear of the numerous advances which had been made, especially in the last five years, in our field. On the evening of my arrival I was telephoned in succession by Dr Ruth Lemcke, Dr Dienes and Dr Wittler. The first had received a grant from the World Health Organization to spend a year in Melbourne with the Mycoplasma scientists there. She had come to New York to the congress on the return journey from Australia and had much to tell me as we had not seen each other for a whole year. The Waldorf-Astoria is an old hotel; it is built in what is known as the 'Victorian style' and so is much more homely than the other giant hotels of the North American Continent in which I have attended congresses, such as the Barbizon Plaza and the Queen Elizabeth Hotel in Montréal. There was also a bible on my bed table and I read each evening from the Old Testament before I went to sleep. This time I met a great number of old friends and acquaintances in New York and made new acquaintances. In particular I made friends with Dr Arthur Grace, from New York, with whom I have since corresponded. Naturally I also saw Dr Dienes frequently. The congress gave a special dinner for him and me in the premises of the New York Academy of Sciences. In a pleasant way it was quite a family affair although very well attended and many witty speeches were made. Professor Harry Morton, Dr Eaton (from the Eaton Agent), Dr Sharp (a collaborator of Dr Dienes), and from London Dr Edward and Dr Lemcke all spoke; of course Dr Dienes and I had to reply. What impressed me especially: there were drinks before the meal, but no wine with the dinner; instead there was a large, good cup of coffee afterwards. We had to walk to and from the Waldorf—to the Academy, because buses and taxis were on strike—and it was raining! But Dr Csonka gave me his arm and took me under his large umbrella.

On the last day of the congress, three young post-graduate students from Yale University asked me to discuss with them a bacteriological problem which gave them difficulties. They were especially nice young people and so it gave me much pleasure. But the best of it was, that they solved *my* problem the next morning very amiably; since buses and taxis were on strike I did not know how to get to the eastern Airways Terminus of Kennedy Airport the next day. They offered to ask a colleague, 'Fritz', the owner of a car to drive us all there. Fritz also brought his little son and all formed an escort for me to my flight to Bogotá. We still had time at the airport for a cup of coffee and then we made our farewells. This was a pleasant conclusion and a pleasant start to my journey to unknown South America.

That is more or less, the story of my life. I would like to quote from the opening speech of the Eighth International Congress for Microbiology, given by Professor E.G.D. Murray. It comes from the English poet and philosopher Sir John Davis, who lived in the 16th century and it runs:

> Skill comes so slow and life so fast doth fly
> We learn so little and forget so much

Last Working Period

Perhaps my readers are astonished that my closing note is somewhat melancholic. But even if I am completely content with old age a slightly sad note slips in, when one looks back on one's life and finds that one wished to do so much and accomplished so little and there is now hardly anything to add to it.

Concluding Remarks

I AM WRITING these concluding lines in 1973, in the eighty-second year of my life, sitting in my quiet, comfortable, familiar room. In the window are my plants and flowers; it is warm here (although it is November) and the sun shines in through my large bay window. There is a feeling of peace within me! Personally, I have every reason to be content, for two conditions apply to my present way of life, conditions which are very important in old age and whose fulfilment I wish for everyone's old age. I am healthy (apart from slight discomforts which can be easily endured) and I have enough money to live simply but comfortably. As I sit in my armchair and write and let my life pass before my inner eye, with its kaleidoscopic images, I have to say: I have experienced very, very sad times but also very satisfying and pleasing times. You might well say that it has been a normal and, on the whole, a good life. I have known despair and have also enjoyed moments of great happiness. One does not write about these moments of despair or heights of happiness. These moments are too personal and remain hidden in the heart.

I have always had good friends; many have gone to their death before me (if only one could see them once again!). But I still have friends. Human relationships and satisfying work are the most important things in life! I am interested in people; those whom I find pleasing and can come to terms with, because we are on the same 'wavelength'. Our beings vibrate in sympathy and produce harmony.

I believe that I have—even if with some difficulty—learned to grow old.

Concluding Remarks

The secret is that one must grasp the fact that the body is old and used up, even if the intellect functions, or is at least 'fifty per cent' functional. One must give in to the body; must allow more rest hours than formerly, never rush, never try to force things. What cannot be done today can be done tomorrow or the day after. One is best cosseted at home; in those hours after resting one is fresh enough to be together with others, to read, to write or to do those things which give one pleasure. One should eat little and exert oneself as little as possible. The imagination can perhaps still take flight and be filled with beautiful happy impressions, but everything else in moderation—that is the golden rule. That brings contentment; over-exertion brings depression.

The world is no ideal place to live in as we experience it today. It must also be remembered that nature is unfeeling. She creates and she destroys and is quite cold and indifferent. I am not religious, in the dogmatic sense. Dogmas are human inventions. What are the laws, the secrets of the universe, of the milky way, of our solar system, of the earth and of our own existence; in the end we do not know despite all the physics, mathematics and all speculation. And I believe that although we know much, the final secret of all things will never be fathomed.

Man differs from the rest of the living world mainly in his capacity for thought; he can even think about mankind, about himself. One may eventually live in harmony with oneself, but not with 'mankind'. By that I mean: the individual can endure and learn from his mistakes (and every man occasionally goes astray, even with the best will in the world!), but can never forgive the mistakes and misdeeds of humanity. Men plunder, rob, hate, despise, etc. their own brethren. They torture and murder each other in the most ferocious and villainous ways. This has taken place over thousands, hundreds of thousands and perhaps even millions of years. We are indeed no better than the former cannibals or headhunters. The longer I have lived the more I have come to realize this and it makes me very sad!

Together with the miracles of, for example, Beethoven's *Fidelio* (how my heart stands still when I hear the trumpet ring out!), Michelangelo's David, together with the most splendid inventions of architecture and many other human masterpieces of the greatest versatility and beauty, together with all this we see almost daily—even if we except murder and slaughter—the growth of envy, jealousy, covetousness, hate, contempt and arrogance. Not only among peoples, societies of all kinds, but even within families. Will it always continue so? Can one at the end of one's life yet see a glimmer of hope? Can one believe that man, with the intelligence that enables him to put a man on the moon, use it to improve the human condition? When we, as children, sang, 'Lovely moon, you pass so quietly through the evening clouds', who could have dreamed that a man's foot would tread there one day? May we now dream that other forms of society will come which are able to improve human conditions?

The terrible atrocities of our time are deeply scored into us and are very disturbing! Perhaps the *lethargy* with which the mass of people allow these horrors to occur is the terrible aspect of the world today. Our children, our youth must be aroused to look at these happenings. Our young people must not hate people of other nations, other beliefs and other state systems, but they should fight to improve society; they must learn neighbourly love, or better, respect for human beings in the widest sense of the phrase, Tolerance—with a capital T, and Supernationalism!

And *yet* despite all the sorrows we are made aware of daily in our time, with the end of my life in prospect in my old age, I have a feeling of contentment.

How does this come about? Everything we have become, all we have achieved in life, has its source in what others—our parents, teachers, brothers and sisters, our fellow beings—have bestowed on us. And we again have contributed something, though it may be little. How many good people have I known, how many have given me their friendship, how many I have revered and loved, and there are still those living with whom I have the best of relationships. Thus a *stream of good* (unwritten and unmarked) flows through the history of mankind. It will go on and will not be lost as long as men live on this earth.

For this, I am grateful and it fills me with hope and confidence.

Publications

Klieneberger, E., 1917. Ueber die Grösse und Beschaffenheit der Zellkerne mit besonderer Berücksichtigung der Systematik. Diss., Frankfurt a/M., 1917. Dresden: C. Heinrich.

Klieneberger, E., 1923. Ueber die Bekämpfung der Pharaoameise. *Dtsch. med. Wschr.* No. 41.

Klieneberger, E., 1923. Eine Hausplage und ihre Bekämpfung. *Umschau, Jahrg.* **27,** Heft 41, 707-708.

Klieneberger, E., 1924. Ueber die Bekämpfung der Pharaoameise. *Verh. dtsch. Ges. angewa. Entomol.* **4,** 83-85.

Klieneberger, E., 1924. Zur Methodik der Prüfung von chemischen Desinfektionsmitteln im Suspensionsversuch. *Z. Hyg. Infekt. -Kr.* **102,** 339-351.

Klieneberger, E., 1925. Die Gasbildung in Zuckeragar (hohe Schicht). *Zbl. Bakt. I. Abt. Orig.* **96,** 181-213.

Klieneberger, E., 1925. Chemische Analyse durch Bakterien. *Umschau, Jahrg.* **29,** 994-995.

Klieneberger, 1927. Ist der gaslose Paratyphus B-Bazillus eine besondere Art? *Zbl. Bakt. I. Abt. Orig.* **101,** 305-311.

Klieneberger, E., 1927. Künstliche Gewinn—und Verluständerungen im Salizin (bw. Arbutin) Vergärungsvermögen eines Colibakteriums in besonders ausgedehnten Versuchsreihen. *Zbl. Bakt. I. Abt. Orig.* **101,** 461-482.

Klieneberger, E., 1927. Die Erzeugung von Modifikationen durch 'spezifischen' Reiz als Mittel der Artcharakterisierung. *Zbl. Bakt. I. Orig.* **104,** 456-459.

Klieneberger, E., 1928. Ueber die Anfertigung von Schimmelpilzpräparaten für Kurszwecke. *Zbl. Bakt. I. Orig.* **108,** 207-209.

Klieneberger, E., 1928. Pankreas und bakteriophagische Wirkung, nebst einem Anhang: eine optimale Methode der Bakteriophagengewinnung. *Z. Immun. -Forsch.* **56,** 32-48.

Klieneberger, E., 1929. Ein Stamm mit eigenartigen Abkömmlingen und der Zusammenhang des Auftretens solcher atypischen Abkömmlinge mit Bakteriophagie und Lysogenität. *Zbl. Bakt. I. Orig.* **112,** 354-368.

Klieneberger, E., Zur Bakterienhaemolyse nach Sonnenschein. *Zbl. Bakt. I. Orig.* **117,** 344-352.

Klieneberger, E., 1930. Der Einfluss verschiedener Salze auf die Wirksamkeit von Bakteriophagensuspensionen, auf ihre Filtrabilität und Adsorbierbarkeit. *Zbl. Bakt. I. Orig.* **118,** 411-422.

Klieneberger, E., 1930. Die Typen in der Influenzabazillengruppe und ihre Verbreitung in der Nachepidemiezeit von März bis Dezember 1929. *Z. Hyg. Infekt. -Kr.* **III,** 1-30.

Klieneberger, E., 1930. Bakterienpleomorphismus und Bakterienentwicklungsgänge. *Ergebn. Hyg. Bakt. etc.* **II,** 499-555. (Med. Habil. -Schr. Frankfurt a/M 1930.)

Klieneberger, E., 1931. Influenzabazillen bei Gesunden nach einer Epidemie. *Zbl. Bakt. Abt. I. Orig.* **121,** 72-75.

Klieneberger, E., 1931. Passage von Bakteriophagen innerhalb des Organismus. *Zbl. Bakt. Abt. I. Orig.* **122,** 168-170. Heft 1/3, Beiheft.

Klieneberger, E., 1931. Die heutigen Auffassungen der verschiedenen Formen der Bakterienzellen einer Art. *Klin. Wschr.* **10,** 481-484.

Klieneberger, E., 1931. Neue Versuche Ph. Hadleys zum Nachweis verusartiger Bakterien-Stadien. *Klin. Wschr.* **10,** 481-484.

Klieneberger, E., 1931. Unsichtbares Leben? In *Natur und Museum*, Heft I, pp. 17-26. Senckenbergische Naturforschende Gesellschaft.

Klieneberger, E., 1931. Die Durchgängigkeit der physiologischen Filter des Organismus für Bakteriophagen. *Naunyn-Schmiedebergs Arch. exp. Path. Pharmak.* **161,** 485-510.

Klieneberger, E., 1932. Die Gewinnung von Bakteriophagen aus Kruse-Sonne Stämmen. *Zbl. Bakt. I. Orig.* **123,** 318-332.

Klieneberger, E., 1932. Ueber die Brauchbarkeit unserer Züchtungsverfahren für bakterielle Umwandlungsstudien. *Zbl. Bakt. Abt. I. Orig.* **123,** 278-286.

Publications

Klieneberger, E., 1934. Mikroben bei Paradentose. Paradentium (Beil. z. zahnärztl. Rdsch.) **6**, Sp. 43-48, 79-84, 103-108.

Klieneberger, E., 1934. The colonial development of the organisms of pleuropneumonia and agalactia on serum agar and variations of the morphology under different conditions of growth. *J. Path. Bact.* **39**, 409-420.

Klieneberger, E., 1935. The natural occurrence of pleuropneumonia-like organisms in apparent symbiosis with *Streptobacillus moniliformis* and other bacteria. *J. Path. Bact.* **40**, 93-105.

Klieneberger, E., 1936. Further studies on *Streptobacillus moniliformis* and its symbiont. *J. Path. Bact.* **42**, 587-598.

Klieneberger, E., and Steabben, D.B., 1937. On a pleuropneumonia-like organism in lung lesions of rats, with notes on the clinical and pathological features of the underlying condition. *J. Hyg.* **37**, 143-152.

Klieneberger, E., 1938. Pleuropneumonia-like organisms of diverse provenance: some results of an enquiry into methods of differentiation. *J. Hyg.* **38**, 458-476.

Findlay, G.M., Klieneberger, E., MacCallum, F.O. and MacKenzie, R.H., 1938. Rolling disease. New syndrome in mice associated with a pleuropneumonia-like organism. *Lancet* **235**, 1511-1513.

Klieneberger, E., 1939. Studies on the pleuropneumonia-like organism. Third Int. Congr. Microbiol., New York, 1939, Abstr. of Communications, pp. 20-21.

Klieneberger, E., 1939. Studies of pleuropneumonia-like organisms: bacteriological features and serological relationships of strains of various sources. *J. Path. Bact.* **49**, 451-452.

Klieneberger, E., 1939. Studies on pleuropneumonia-like organisms: the L 4 organism as the cause of Woglom's 'pyogenic virus'. *J. Hyg.* **39**, 260-265.

Findlay, G.M., Klieneberger, E., MacCallum, F.O. and MacKenzie, R.D., 1939. Eperthrozoon in the blood of mice and its possible relationship to pleuropneumonia-like organisms. *Trans. Roy. Soc. Trop. Med. Hyg.* **33**, 6-7.

Findlay, G.M., MacKenzie, R.D., MacCallum, F.O. and Klieneberger, E., 1939. The aetiology of Polyarthritis in the rat. *Lancet* **237**, 7-10.

Klieneberger, E., 1940. The pleuropneumonia-like organisms: further comparative studies and a descriptive account of recently discovered types. *J. Hyg.* **40**, 204-222.

Klieneberger, E. and Steabben, D.B., 1940. On the association of the pleuropneumonia-like organism L 3 with bronchiectatic lesions in rats. *J. Hyg.* **40,** 223-227.

Partridge, S. M. and Klieneberger, E., 1941. Isolation of cholesterol from the oily droplets found in association with the L 1 organism separated from *Streptobacillus moniliformis. J. Path. Bact.* **52,** 219-223.

Klieneberger, E., 1942. Some new observations bearing on the nature of the pleuropneumonia-like organism known as L 1 associated with *Streptobacillus moniliformis. J. Hyg.* **42,** 485-497.

Klieneberger, E. and Smiles, J., 1942. Some new observations on the developmental cycle of the organisms of bovine pleuropneumonia and related microbes. *J. Hyg.* **42,** 110-123.

Klieneberger-Nobel, E., 1944. Changes in the nuclear structure of bacteria during spore formation. *J. Path. Bact.* **56,** 286-287.

Klieneberger-Nobel, E., 1945. Pleuropneumonia-like organisms in the human vagina. *Lancet,* **249,** 46-47.

Klieneberger-Nobel, E., 1945. Changes in the nuclear structure of bacteria, particularly during spore formation. *J. Hyg.* **44,** 99-108.

Klieneberger-Nobel, E., 1947. Isolation and maintenance of an L 1-like culture from *Fusiformis necrophorus* (syn. *Bact. Funduliforme, Bacteroides funduliformes). J. Hyg.* **45,** 407-409.

Klieneberger-Nobel, E., 1947. Morphological appearances of various stages in *B. proteus* and *coli. J. Hyg.* **45,** 410-412.

Klieneberger-Nobel, E., 1947. Chromatinstrukturen der Bakterien und ihre biologische Bedeutung. *Schweiz. Z. Path. Bakt.* **10,** 480-487.

Klieneberger-Nobel, E., 1947. The life cycle of sporing actinomyces as revealed by a study of their structure and septation. *J.gen. Microbiol.* **1,** 22-32.

Klieneberger-Nobel, E., 1947. A cytological study of myxococci. *J. gen. Microbiol.* **1,** 33-38.

Klieneberger-Nobel, E., 1948. Ueber Kapsel- und Schleimbildung bei Bakterien. *Schweiz. z. Path. Bakt.* **11,** 336-345.

Klieneberger-Nobel, E., 1948. Capsules and mucoid envelopes of bacteria. *J. Hyg.* **46,** 345-348.

Klieneberger-Nobel, E., 1948. Sur les changements de structure du noyau pendant la formation de la spore. *C.R. Soc. Biol.* **142,** 1276-1277.

Klieneberger-Nobel, E., 1949. On *Streptobacillus moniliformis* and the filterability of its L-form. *J. Hyg.* **47,** 393-395.

Publications

Klieneberger-Nobel, E., 1949. Origin, development and significance of L-forms in bacterial cultures. *J. gen. Microbiol.* **3,** 434-443.

Klieneberger-Nobel, E., 1950. Methods for the study of the cytology of bacteria and pleuropneumonia-like organisms. *Q. J. Micr. Sci.* (3rd. ser.) **91,** 340-347.

Klieneberger-Nobel, E., 1951. Filterable forms of bacteria. *Bact. Rev.* **15,** 77-103.

Klieneberger-Nobel, E., 1951. The L—cycle: a process of regeneration in bacteria. *J. gen. Microbiol.* **5,** 525-530.

Klieneberger-Nobel, E., 1953. Filterable forms of bacteria (including L-forms). Atti del VI Congresso Internazionale de Microbiologia, Roma, 1, pp. 128-133.

Klieneberger-Nobel, E., 1954. La distinction entre les organism du groupe de la Pleuropneumonie et la phase L des Bactéries. Leur Relation possible avec les virus. In *Problèmes actuels de Virologie,* (P. Hauduroy, et al., eds) pp. 58-66. Paris: Masson.

Klieneberger-Nobel, E., 1954. Micro-organisms of the pleuropneumonia group. *Biol. Rev.* **29,** 154-184.

Klieneberger-Nobel, E., 1954. Micro-organisms of the pleuropneumonia group, their nature, pathogenicity and modes of infection in relation to their possible harmfulness in human genito-urinary disease. World Health Organization, Symposium on non-gonococcal urethritis, Monaco 1954, WHO (VDT) 115 (Masch. schr. vervielf.).

Klieneberger-Nobel, E. and Cheng, K., -K., 1955. On the association of the pleuropneumonia-like organism with experimentally produced bronchiectasis in rats. *J. Path. Bact.* **70,** 245-246.

Klieneberger-Nobel, E. and Cuckow, F.W., 1955. A study of organisms of the pleuropneumonia group by electron microscopy. *J. gen. Microbiol.* **12,** 95-99.

Cuckow, F.W. and Klieneberger-Nobel, E., 1955. Further studies of organisms of the pleuropneumonia group by electron microscopy. *J. gen. Microbiol.* **13,** 149-154.

Klieneberger-Nobel, E., 1956. Ueber die Wesensverschiedenheit der peripneumonie-ähnlichen Organismen und der L-Phase der Bakterien. *Zbl. Abt. I. Bakt. Orig.* **165,** 329-343.

Klieneberger-Nobel, E., 1957. Microorganisms du groupe pleuropneumonique, nature, pouvoir pathogène et modes d'infection du point de vue du danger qu'ils peuvent représenter dans les maladies génito-urinaires de l'homme. In *Bibliothèque de l'Union Internationale contre le Péril Vénérien et les Tréponematoses,* No. 1, p. 43. Paris: Masson.

Klieneberger-Nobel, E., 1958. L-Formen der Bakterien. (Bericht üb.d. Oesterr. Ges. Mikrobiol. u. Hyg., 1958 a. d. Semmering b. Wien) *Zbl. Bakt. I. Abt. Ref.* **169,** 353-355.

Klieneberger-Nobel, E., 1958. Die L-Form der Bakterien. *Zbl. Bakt. I. Abt. Orig.* **173,** 376-385.

Brenner, S., Dark, F.A., Gerhardt, P., Jeynes, M.H., Kandler, O., Kellenberger, E., Klieneberger-Nobel, E., McQuillen, K., Rubio-Huertos, M., Salton, M.R.J., Strange, R.E., Tomcsik, J. and Weibull, C., 1958. Bacterial protoplasts. *Nature,* **181,** 1713-1715.

Klieneberger-Nobel, E., 1959. Pleuropneumonia-like organisms in genital infections. *Brit. med. J.* **1,** 19-23.

Klieneberger-Nobel, E., 1959. Possible significance of PPLO in human genital infection. *Brit. J. Vener. Dis.* **35,** 20-23.

Klieneberger-Nobel, E., 1960. Pathogenicity and immunology of organisms of the pleuropneumonia group. *Ann. N.Y. Acad. Sci.* **79,** 615-625.

Klieneberger-Nobel, E., 1960. L-Forms of bacteria. In *The Bacteria. A Treatise on Structure and Function* (I.C. Gunsalus and R.Y. Stanier, eds) Vol. I., pp. 361-386. New York and London: Academic Press.

Klieneberger-Nobel, E., 1961. Die peripneumonie-ähnlichen Organismen (PPLO, Mycoplasmataceae), ihre Züchtung, Morphologie, Serologie und Pathogenität. *Klin. Wschr.* **39,** 661-667.

Klieneberger-Nobel, E., 1962. *Pleuropneumonia-like organisms (PPLO) Mycoplasmataceae.* London and New York: Academic Press.

Klieneberger-Nobel, E., Some current trends in the field of PPLO. *Recent Progr. Microbiol.* **8,** 504-510.

Klieneberger-Nobel, E., 1965. *Focus on Bacteria.* London and New York: Academic Press.

Klieneberger-Nobel, E., Mycoplasmas, a brief historical review. *Ann. N.Y. Acad. Sci.* 713.

Klieneberger-Nobel, E., 1969. Mycoplasmataceae. In *Die Infektionskrankheiten des Menschen und ihre Erreger.* (A. Grumbach and O. Bonin, eds) Vol. 1, pp. 274-283; Vol. 2, pp. 1283-1292. Stuttgart: Georg Thieme.

Klieneberger-Nobel, E., 1969. Foreword. In *The Mycoplasmatales and the L-phase of bacteria* (L. Hayflick, ed.). New York: Appleton-Century-Crofts.

Klieneberger-Nobel, E., 1970. Hundert Jahre Professor Max Neisser. *Zbl. Bakt. I. Abt. Orig.* **215,** 279-285.

Publications

Klieneberger-Nobel, E., 1977. *Pionierleistüngen für die Medizinische Mikrobiologie, Lebenserinnerungen.* Stuttgart and New York: Gustav Fischer Verlag.

RAYMOND H. FOGLER LIBRARY